COUNTRIES OF THE WORLD

Spain

Gareth Stevens Publishing
A WORLD ALMANAC EDUCATION GROUP COMPANY

About the Author: Katherine Grinsted has degrees in English and History as well as in Journalism. She is an Australian travel writer and has written for books, magazines, and television programs in Australia, England, and Singapore. She has worked on several children's television shows as well as many adult education BBC programs. A big fan of *paella* and *sangría*, she has greatly enjoyed her travels through Europe.

PICTURE CREDITS

Archive Photos: 82, 83
Bes Stock: 91
Camera Press: 14 (top), 15 (top), 37 (top),
   65, 66 (both), 84 (right)
Sylvia Cordaiy: 54, 55, 73
DDB Stock Photo: 58, 67
Focus Team — Italy: Cover, 2, 5, 31 (top),
   36, 44, 57, 77
Haga Library Inc., Japan: 3 (center), 4, 18,
   27 (bottom), 38, 42, 46, 56, 61
HBL Network Photo Agency: 1, 3 (bottom),
   6, 8, 10, 14 (bottom), 19, 26, 27 (top), 30,
   32, 33, 39, 40, 41, 43, 47, 50, 60, 64, 89
Hutchison Library: 75, 78
Illustrated London News Picture Library:
   15 (bottom)
International Photobank: 81
North Wind Picture Archives: 11, 12,
   15 (center), 29, 51, 52, 71, 76, 80
Christine Osborne: 16, 31 (bottom)
Chip and Rosa Maria de la Cueva
   Peterson: 7, 20, 25, 28, 63, 74, 79
David Simpson: 3 (top), 17, 22, 23, 24,
   34, 35, 37 (bottom), 48, 49, 62 (both), 69
Still Pictures: 9 (both)
Tan Chung Lee: 53
Topham Picturepoint: 13, 45, 59, 70, 72,
   84 (left), 85
Travel Ink: 87
Trip Photographic Library: 21, 68

Digital Scanning by Superskill Graphics Pte Ltd

Written by
KATHERINE GRINSTED

Edited by
AYESHA ERCELAWN

Designed by
LOO CHUAN MING

Picture research by
SUSAN JANE MANUEL

First published in North America in 1999 by
Gareth Stevens Publishing
A World Almanac Education Group Company
330 West Olive Street, Suite 100
Milwaukee, Wisconsin 53212 USA

For a free color catalog describing
Gareth Stevens' list of high-quality books
and multimedia programs, call
1-800-542-2595 (USA) or
1-800-461-9120 (CANADA).
Gareth Stevens Publishing's
Fax: (414) 332-3567.

© **TIMES EDITIONS PTE LTD 1999**
© **TIMES MEDIA PRIVATE LIMITED 2001**
Originated and designed by
Times Editions
An imprint of Times Media Private Limited
A member of the Times Publishing Group
Times Centre, 1 New Industrial Road
Singapore 536196
http://www.timesone.com.sg/te

Library of Congress Cataloging-in-Publication Data
Grinsted, Katherine.
Spain / by Katherine Grinsted.
   p.   cm. -- (Countries of the world)
Includes bibliographical references and index.
Summary: An overview of the third largest country in Europe including information about its geography, history, government, current issues, and many aspects of the lifestyle of its people.
ISBN 0-8368-2312-5 (lib. bdg.)
1. Spain--Juvenile literature. [1. Spain.] I. Title.
II. Series: Countries of the world (Milwaukee, Wis.)
DP17.G75   1999
946--dc21   98-54202

Printed in Singapore

3 4 5 6 7 8 9 07 06 05 04 03 02 01

Contents

AN OVERVIEW OF SPAIN

The third largest country in Europe, Spain has a stunning landscape of rugged mountains, barren plateaus, fertile riverbanks, and beautiful beaches. It is a bridge to the continent of Africa, with Morocco to the south across the Strait of Gibraltar.

The nation has a remarkable history. The Spanish empire once stretched across the globe and left its legacy throughout the New World. An accessible bridge to Europe for invasions by North African Muslims, Spain endured almost eight hundred years of Islamic rule starting from the eighth century. Today, the country is a blend of the different ethnic groups that have settled there over the centuries. The official language is Castilian Spanish, but other languages are spoken regionally.

Opposite: **Spanish architect Antonio Gaudí designed the famous church of the Sagrada Família in Barcelona.**

Below: Ferias **(feh-REE-uhs) are outdoor markets for people buying and selling horses or bulls. Never letting a good crowd go to waste, Spaniards turn these markets into fun fiestas of parading, singing, and dancing.**

THE FLAG OF SPAIN

According to legend, the Spanish flag dates back to the ninth century, when the king of France, Charles II (also known as Charles the Bald), wiped bloodstained fingers down the Count of Aragón's shield. Stripes were being used in the Aragón flag by the twelfth century and have been used in the national flag of Spain almost continuously since 1795. The dictator Francisco Franco added a new coat of arms in 1936, but this was dropped in 1981. The flag today combines the coats of arms of León, Castile, Navarra, and Aragón into one shield.

Geography

Spain is the third largest country in Europe. It covers 194,898 square miles (504,785 square kilometers), which makes it smaller than Texas but larger than California. Spain occupies most of the Iberian Peninsula, the name for the southwestern tip of Europe. To the north of Spain lie France, Andorra, and the Bay of Biscay. The Pyrenees mountain range forms a natural northern border. To the south lie the Atlantic Ocean, the Mediterranean Sea, and the Strait of Gibraltar separating Spain from Africa. To the west lie Portugal and the Atlantic Ocean, and, to the east, the Spanish coastline meets the Mediterranean Sea. The sandy beaches of the Mediterranean are a contrast to Spain's northern and western coastline, where rocky cliffs and coves face the Atlantic Ocean.

Spain's territory also includes two groups of islands — the Canary Islands in the Atlantic Ocean and the Balearic Islands in the Mediterranean Sea. Only seven of the Canary Islands are inhabited, the main one being Tenerife. Majorca, Minorca, Ibiza, Formentera, and Cabrera form the Balearic Islands.

TERRITORIES IN AFRICA

Spain has two small territories on the northern coast of Africa — Ceuta and Melilla. They have belonged to Spain since the sixteenth century. Both port towns border Morocco.
(A Closer Look, page 72)

Below: Forming a natural wall between France and Spain, the Pyrenees protected many early Spanish civilizations from European invaders.

After Switzerland, Spain is the most mountainous country in Europe, with an average altitude of 2,130 feet (650 m). The Pyrenees extend along Spain's northern border. The Cantabrian Mountains are in the northwest, Sierra de Guadarrama runs across central Spain, and the snowcapped peaks of Sierra Nevada and Sierra Morena are in the south. Spain's tallest mountain, Pico de Teide, which rises 12,198 feet (3,718 m), is on the island of Tenerife. At 11,411 feet (3,478 m), Pico de Mulhacén is the highest point on the Spanish mainland.

Between these mountain ranges, there is a large, almost treeless central plateau called the Meseta. Fertile lowland areas lie near both coasts, especially along the Mediterranean coast. Coursing through the Meseta, mountains, and lowlands of Spain are some of the longest rivers in Europe. The Ebro, Spain's longest river, flows through northeastern Spain for 565 miles (910 kilometers) before emptying into the Mediterranean Sea. The Tagus runs west, from its source in the Iberian Mountains all the way to the Atlantic coast of Portugal. The Guadalquivir River, flowing through the fertile south, is the deepest river in Spain.

Above: **Southern Spain faces the Atlantic Ocean and the Mediterranean Sea. The Strait of Gibraltar connects these two bodies of water.**

Climate

The rugged landscape of Spain has resulted in a range of temperatures and climates. The Cantabrian Mountains create a strong dividing line between climatic zones. The area known as "green Spain," composed of the Basque Country, Cantabria, Asturias, and Galicia, lies to the north of this range. Here, winters are mild and summers cool because winds off the Atlantic Ocean bring frequent rainfall and prevent temperature extremes. For example, San Sebastián has temperatures that range from an average of 74° Fahrenheit (23° Centigrade) in the summer months of July and August to 46° F (8° C) in winter.

To the south of the Cantabrian Mountains lies "dry Spain." Most of the central Meseta gets little rainfall, and drought is common in summer. The winters are usually bitter, with heavy snowfall and biting winds. In Madrid, the winter cold is sufficient to freeze surrounding streams, while summer temperatures in Seville can rise as high as 120° F (49° C).

The Mediterranean coast is also quite dry, with hot summers and mild, wet winters. Refreshing sea breezes and the occasional thunderstorm cool the summer heat on the northern end of the coast. The southern Mediterranean coast has a more subtropical climate, and the occasional hot, dry wind blows in from Africa.

Above: Andalusia, in southern Spain, has a highly varied landscape, with dry, desert land near the coast in striking contrast to fertile plains and mountains farther inland.

DOÑANA NATIONAL PARK

Protected since 1969, this beautiful wetland reserve in southern Spain is an important stopping place for migratory birds flying from Europe to Africa in winter.

(A Closer Look, page 54)

Plants and Animals

Varying climates and topography have resulted in a diversity of plant life across Spain. The mountains of the north and west have grassy valleys with woods of poplars and evergreen oaks. Extensive forests of larch and fir cover the higher slopes. The central plains and mountains of southern Spain are mostly covered with tough bushes, thorny shrubs, and herbs. The main tree found in these regions is the cork oak, from which the bark is stripped every ten years and used for cork. The cultivation of olive trees is also a major agricultural activity. Similarly, grapes are grown throughout Spain except in the northern Basque Country. Palm trees, sugarcane, oranges, lemons, figs, almonds, and chestnuts grow along the Mediterranean coast. In contrast, the landscape of southeastern Spain is primarily desert.

Above and *below:* **The most likely place to see rare animals, such as the European wolf** *(above)* **or griffon vultures** *(below)*, **is in one of Spain's national parks.**

Rabbits and partridge are the most common wildlife in Spain; much rarer are lynx, wildcats, wolves, foxes, wild boars, wild goats, and deer. Bird life is very rich and includes the rare golden eagle. Spain's mountain lakes and streams are home to fish such as trout and barbel. Deep-sea aquatic life includes tuna, sardines, and dolphins (found off the Atlantic coast), as well as octopuses and squid (found off the Mediterranean coast).

History

The earliest records of human habitation in Spain are Stone Age cave paintings in the northern mountains. Between 800 and 500 B.C., various civilizations found their way to what is now Spain. The Phoenicians and Greeks came from the east, sailing across the Mediterranean Sea before reaching southern coastal Spain and the Balearic Islands. The Iberians, a North African people, arrived from the south, and their culture quickly spread throughout the peninsula. The Celts arrived overland from the north.

By the third century B.C., the African state of Carthage had settled southern Spain. After the Romans conquered Carthage in 202 B.C., the peninsula became a province of the Roman Empire known as Hispania. The Western Roman Empire crumbled in the late fifth century A.D., and the Visigoths, a Germanic tribe, took over and later established the Catholic faith as the official state religion.

The Moors

In 711, a Berber Muslim army invaded from North Africa and, over the next eight years, conquered most of Spain. The new rulers became known as the Moors. Many Spaniards converted to Islam, and Moorish culture flourished for nearly three hundred years. The Muslim rulers' capital was established at Córdoba, and

Left: The Alhambra, in Granada, is one of the finest examples of Moorish architecture. The palace complex has a series of pools, graceful patios and gardens, and intricately carved stonework and mosaics.

CHRISTOPHER COLUMBUS

In 1492, Christopher Columbus set sail, with the backing of Ferdinand and Isabella, to find a new route to Asia. En route, he accidentally arrived at the Caribbean islands and made them Spanish colonies, setting the stage for Spanish expansion into North and South America.

(A Closer Look, page 50)

Left: Christopher Columbus discusses his journey with Queen Isabella and King Ferdinand.

Andalusia, or al-Andalus, became a thriving region of trade and prosperous cities. The sciences, such as astronomy, chemistry, and medicine, flourished along with the arts.

A small area of Christian rule survived in the north, however. In the eleventh century, the Christian reconquest of Spain began, and Christian kings joined forces to win back much of Spain from the Muslims. Navarra, Aragón (which included Catalonia), Asturias, and Castile became important independent kingdoms.

Ferdinand and Isabella

The origins of modern Spain can be traced to 1469 and the marriage of Isabella I of Castile to Ferdinand II of Aragón. By joining their two kingdoms, Isabella and Ferdinand paved the way for Spain's future success.

The year 1492 was a pivotal one. With the conquest of Granada, the new Spanish army completed the expulsion of the Moors. In the same year, Christopher Columbus set sail on a journey of discovery that led to the conquest of the New World and the start of the Spanish empire.

Spain as a World Power

Spain was also expanding its control throughout Europe. In 1512, the kingdom of Navarra became part of the unified kingdom of Spain. Spanish culture flourished, and Spain became a major world power. The grandson of Ferdinand and Isabella, Charles I, inherited the Spanish throne at the age of seventeen. He also inherited the crowns of Germany, Austria, and the Netherlands. Appointed Holy Roman Emperor Charles V, he became the most powerful ruler in Europe. Spain also controlled much of the New World during his reign.

The Spanish empire was at its height until 1588, when the Spanish fleet of ships known as the Armada was defeated by the English navy. Spain began a slow decline. After the War of the Spanish Succession (1701–1714) with England and Austria over the throne, King Philip V lost most of Spain's other holdings in Europe. The British annexed Gibraltar and Minorca in 1713. In 1808, Napoleon Bonaparte of France put his brother on the throne of Spain. It took the combined forces of Spain, England, and Portugal to finally drive the French out of Spain in 1814.

Between 1810 and 1825 most of Spain's American colonies won their independence, and in 1898, after losing the Spanish–American War, Spain lost the rest of its important overseas territories, including Cuba, Puerto Rico, the Philippines, and Guam.

THE SPANISH ARMADA

Spain's decline as an empire began when the English navy defeated its fleet of ships known as the Armada in 1588. With longer-range firepower and faster ships, the English sailors easily outmaneuvered the Spanish ships.
(A Closer Look, page 70)

Below: Isabella and Ferdinand were also known as the Catholic Monarchs. They formed the Spanish Inquisition, which killed or imprisoned people who did not strictly follow the Catholic faith. Many Jews were executed or expelled from Spain.

Left: **The Spanish Civil War raged from 1936 to 1939. Germany and Italy got involved on the side of the Nationalists. The Soviet Union, France, and Mexico helped the Republicans. The Nationalists, under the command of General Franco, won the war.**

Troubled Times

In the early twentieth century, Spain was one of Europe's poorest countries. It was also in political trouble. In 1931, King Alfonso XIII fled the country, and Spain became a republic. After a general election, republicans, socialists, liberals, and other small parties formed a government, but unrest continued.

The Catalans demanded self-government, monarchists opposed republicans, and poverty in the country was made worse by a worldwide economic depression. In 1936, the Popular Front, an alliance between republicans, socialists, and communists, won the general election. The military, led by General Francisco Franco, revolted. The Spanish Civil War began.

The Civil War raged for nearly three years, with fierce fighting between the Republicans and the Nationalists (the army). In the end, the discipline of the military forces won the day. Madrid fell on March 28, 1939, and, on April 1, General Franco declared the war officially over and himself chief of state.

Under Franco

General Franco ruled Spain until his death in 1975. For thirty-six years, the country was under a military dictatorship. Stability was restored, but the price was individual freedom. During the 1950s and 1960s, Franco finally relaxed his hard-line rule and allowed his regime to become more liberal. This encouraged a period of economic growth, and, by the end of the 1960s, Spain had joined the ranks of industrialized nations.

A Parliamentary Monarchy

When Franco died in 1975, Juan Carlos, grandson of Alfonso XIII, took the oath as king of Spain and promised the people a rapid democratic process to set up a "monarchy for all the Spanish people." Adolfo Suárez González became prime minister. In 1978, the people voted in a new constitution, and a parliamentary monarchy was established. The new constitution recognized that Spain is made up of regions of many nationalities and languages.

Felipe González Márquez, elected prime minister in 1982, continued democratic reforms. In the 1980s, Spain joined the North Atlantic Treaty Organization (NATO) and the European Community. Since the last general election in March 1996, power has been in the hands of a government headed by the conservative Popular Party. Their leader, José María Aznar, is the current prime minister.

Above: **Juan Carlos became king of Spain on November 22, 1975, after the death of Francisco Franco. He had an important goal — to restore democracy in Spain. He sponsored the writing of a new constitution, which was adopted in 1978, and established a parliamentary monarchy in Spain.**

Left: **Madrid's magnificent royal palace was built in the eighteenth century. The present king, Juan Carlos, no longer lives in it, but the palace is still used for state occasions.**

Queen Isabella I (1451–1504)

Isabella I was queen of Castile. She was known as the Catholic queen because of her great support for the Catholic Church. She was also the chief sponsor of the voyages of Christopher Columbus. In 1469, she married Ferdinand II of Aragón, also known as Ferdinand V of Castile. Within ten years, they had united their kingdoms. Isabella's husband was also a fierce Catholic, and together they banned all religions other than Roman Catholicism. Isabella died in 1504, and when Ferdinand died in 1516, the crown passed to their grandson Charles.

Isabella I

Charles I (Holy Roman Emperor Charles V)

Charles was born on February 24, 1500, in the Netherlands. He was the son of Joanna, daughter of Ferdinand and Isabella. Charles did not see Spain until he was seventeen years old, although he inherited the crown of the Spanish kingdom of Castile when he was only six. At the same age, he became king of the Netherlands. When Ferdinand died in 1516, Charles became king of Spain. Only then did he move to Spain and set up his court.

Charles' power increased dramatically when he was crowned Holy Roman Emperor Charles V. His kingdom now spread over much of Europe and across the Atlantic into the Americas. Charles was a great warrior and led his army to victory many times throughout his reign.

Charles I

General Francisco Franco (1892–1975)

General Franco was the authoritarian ruler who governed Spain from 1939 to 1975. After graduating from the Infantry Academy in Toledo in 1910, he rose rapidly in the military ranks and became chief of staff of the Spanish Army in 1935.

In July 1936, Franco joined other right-wing officers in a revolt against the leftist government of Spain. In October, the Nationalist rebels appointed him commander in chief and head of state of their new regime. After three years of waging a bloody civil war against the republic, the Nationalists achieved a complete victory on April 1, 1939. Franco ruled with a heavy hand; tens of thousands of executions during the civil war and its aftermath helped him stay in power. In 1947, Franco reestablished Spain as a monarchy, with himself at the head.

Francisco Franco

Government and the Economy

Government

In 1978, Spain voted for a national constitution that set up a parliamentary monarchy. This means that the monarch, who earns the right to rule by birth, is the official head of state and the commander in chief of the armed forces. However, real power rests with the democratically elected prime minister, who is the head of government.

The parliament consists of two houses. The 350 members of the Congress of Deputies are elected to a four-year term by general vote under a system of proportional representation. The number of deputies from each of the fifty provinces is based on the population. There is also a Senate of 208 directly elected

Below: **The Congreso de los Diputados, or the Congress of Deputies, is one of the two houses of parliament. It is located in the capital, Madrid.**

members and 47 special regional representatives. The senators also serve a four-year term. Each of the forty-seven mainland provinces elects four senators; another twenty senators come from the Balearic Islands, the Canary Islands, Ceuta, and Melilla. The voting age is eighteen.

At the regional level, Spain is divided into fifty provinces within seventeen self-governing regions. Each region has an elected legislative assembly led by a local president. Each province has an appointed governor and an elected council. The provinces are further divided into more than eight thousand municipalities; these are governed by an elected council and a mayor.

The General Council of Judicial Power presides over the judicial system in Spain. The country's highest tribunal is the Supreme Court of Justice in Madrid. Each region and province has a high court, and several lower courts handle penal, labor, and juvenile matters. The other important court is the Constitutional Court, which protects the constitution and judges whether legislation is in accordance with the constitution.

Since its first treaty in 1953, Spain has maintained close defense ties with the United States, which keeps a military base in the country. In 1982, Spain became a member of the North Atlantic Treaty Organization (NATO). There is compulsory military service of nine months for men between twenty-one and thirty-five years of age.

Above: Spain has many political parties. The two major groups are the Spanish Socialist Workers' Party (PSOE) and the Popular Party. Other significant parties include the United Left (a coalition of left-wing parties) and the Catalan and Basque nationalist parties.

THE BASQUE REGION

Despite being given increasing autonomy, internal unrest in Spain still centers on the issue of a separate state for the Basque region. Violence and acts of terrorism by the Basque Homeland and Freedom movement, a Basque separatist organization, caused the deaths of more than eight hundred people between 1968 and 1993.

(A Closer Look, page 44)

Agriculture

Agriculture is an important part of the Spanish economy. Farming, forestry, and fishing employ about 10 percent of the labor force. The main crops are grapes for making wine and olives for making olive oil. Wheat, oranges, and almonds are other important crops.

Spanish farmers are careful to choose crops that can grow in the dry climate. Grapes, olives, and wheat are grown in areas without much water. Irrigation systems are in place for other crops, such as citrus trees, rice, and vegetables. Government projects to provide water for farmers include hydroelectric plants, particularly in the valley of the Ebro River. Farmers also raise livestock, especially sheep and goats.

Forestry and fishing are also important. The cork oak is stripped of its bark to make cork, particularly for wine bottles. The annual catch of fish consists mainly of tuna, mussels, sardines, and squid.

Spain has been a member of the former European Community (now the European Union, or EU) since 1986. Spain provides a large amount of farm produce to western Europe.

Above: **Olive trees are planted across huge areas of Andalusia. The fruit is usually harvested in the winter and pressed for its oil or pickled in brine.**

LA RIOJA AND WINEMAKING

Spain is one of the world's leading winemakers. The mountainous region of La Rioja is a major winemaking area. Vineyards cover the entire region, particularly in the Ebro River valley.
(A Closer Look, page 64)

Industry

Spain began a program of industrial growth in the mid-1950s. The economy continued to expand through the 1960s. When the late 1970s saw an economic slowdown because of rising oil costs and increased imports, the government changed focus and concentrated on developing the steel, shipbuilding, textile, and mining industries. Among the most important manufactured goods in Spain today are cloth, iron and steel, motor vehicles, ships, and clothes. Spain also has vast mineral resources, including coal, iron ore, zinc, lead, copper, mercury, and gypsum.

The European Union, the United States, and Japan are Spain's main trading partners. The country's chief imports include crude petroleum, electronics, and food. Exports include food products, cloth, jewelry, cars, metals, chemicals, minerals, and textiles.

Tourism

Tourism is another important industry in Spain. Most tourists visit the big resort towns along the Mediterranean coast. Spain's warm climate, sandy beaches, and interesting historical sites attract more than 65 million tourists each year.

Below: **Barcelona is Spain's second largest city and one of the busiest ports on the Mediterranean Sea.**

People and Lifestyle

The population of Spain is 40 million. The people are a blend of the original inhabitants of the Iberian Peninsula and the various groups who arrived there over the centuries, including the Phoenicians, Romans, Visigoths, and Moors.

Many of the ethnic groups in Spain have kept a separate cultural identity, maintaining their own language and traditions. These include the Catalans (16 percent of the population), who live mainly in the northeast and on the eastern islands; the Galicians (8 percent), who live in northwestern Spain; the Basques

(4 percent), who live mostly around the Bay of Biscay; and the nomadic Spanish Gypsies (less than 1 percent).

The twentieth century has seen the rapid growth of cities as people looking for work move to urban areas from the countryside. Today, just over 11 percent of Spaniards live in rural areas, compared to 75 percent in 1930. The central plateau, or Meseta, is thinly populated, apart from the crowded Madrid area. Most people live in the coastal territories, particularly in the Basque Country, Catalonia, Valencia, and the Canary and Balearic islands.

Above: **These boys live in Toledo, a city in central Spain.**

Family Life

The family unit is very important in Spanish society, mainly because of the strong influence of Catholicism. Men play a dominant role in the family. As in other traditional and strongly religious societies, women tend to stay in the home and look after the family, although these conventional roles are slowly changing. Traditionally, families are large. Although two-children families have become more common in recent years, the extended family bond remains strong, and grandparents, aunts, uncles, and cousins may live in the same house or nearby. Large family gatherings are frequent. Young people, especially girls, often live at home until they get married and even then will still live close by.

Left: **Small families are becoming increasingly common in Spain. This family of four takes a stroll in the evening, a typical Spanish pastime.**

GYPSIES

Gypsies have lived in Spain since the early fifteenth century. While some continue to lead traditional nomadic lives, others have been assimilated into the mainstream. Although the government has launched programs to better educate and integrate Gypsies, it has also promised to help preserve their traditions.
(A Closer Look, page 58)

21

City Life

Spain's largest cities, Madrid and Barcelona, contain one-fourth of the country's total population. Most city-dwellers live in apartments. Many of these were built on the outskirts of cities during the industrial boom in the 1960s, when people from the countryside flocked to the cities for work. Although these apartments are an important source of cheap and affordable homes, many of these so-called "dormitory towns" were built in a hurry and are badly planned. So if they can afford to, Spaniards prefer to live in newer buildings in the center of town. Living standards in Spain have risen in recent years, and about 70 percent of families own their own home.

However, the fast growth of the cities has created many problems, such as severe traffic congestion and air pollution. Unemployment and crime rates have risen. The greatest toll is on the youth. The small apartments they call home are old and poorly designed, so they do little there except eat and sleep. Parental and religious pressures often make them rebel. Drugs and homelessness have become serious issues.

Below: **Most of the population lives in cities. People still have strong links, however, to the village or region they left behind and often visit their family on weekends or holidays.**

22

Rural Life

In northern Spain, fertile land is divided into family-run farms. Families live on their own land, and their nearest neighbor is relatively far away. In the dry heartland, farms are larger, and people live in villages or small towns. In southern Spain, farmers work and live on huge estates.

Most rural families follow a traditional way of life. They live in whitewashed clay or stone houses and observe many old customs. Changes in lifestyle are taking place, however, as more and more people move to the cities.

Time for a Siesta?

A typical Spanish day used to follow a pattern designed for life in warmer climates. Workers and schoolchildren went home in the afternoon for their main meal of the day, followed by a siesta, or afternoon nap. They would then return to work until late in the evening and did not have their evening meal until after 10 p.m. This pattern of life is slowly changing as the government and employers strive to bring Spain in line with other Western nations, which have a continuous eight-hour workday.

Above: **Small, traditional farms dot Galicia, the greenest region of Spain. Galicians, who are of Celtic origin, speak a language called Gallego and are very proud of their language and culture.**

Left: In an increasingly competitive world, most Spanish children are encouraged to go as far as possible in the education system. This has led to a dramatic rise in the literacy rate. At the turn of the twentieth century, only about 40 percent of Spaniards were literate. Today, that number has risen to 97 percent of people over fourteen years old.

Education

Education in Spain is compulsory for children between the ages of six and fourteen. Government-run schools are free. Some parents enroll their children in the private, Roman Catholic school system. Government grants are also available for students who attend private schools.

Primary education is from ages six to twelve, secondary education from ages twelve to sixteen. At the end of secondary schooling, students take a major exam, and those who pass receive a diploma. Spanish students have to repeat any year of school in which they get poor grades.

THE CHANGING ROLE OF WOMEN

As a result of compulsory school attendance and the industrialization of Spain in the 1960s, the role of women in society has changed considerably. More than 40 percent are in the job force today and many work in jobs once reserved for men.

(*A Closer Look*, page 48)

Many children go home for lunch and a siesta between 1 and 3 p.m., after which they return to class until 5 p.m. This makes the school day a long one, but Spanish children get long holidays, too. They have a three-month vacation during the hot summer months, two to three weeks at Christmas, two weeks at Easter, and several other religious holidays or feast days throughout the year.

After completing their compulsory education, students may take either a vocational training course for one or two years, or a two-year diploma course. They can then take a one-year course in preparation for university entrance.

Left: **Students of Salamanca University. Founded in the thirteenth century, this is one of Europe's oldest and most renowned universities.**

Universities

The university system has three parts. The first three years lead to a basic degree. A further two or three years leads to a higher degree. Students wanting to earn a doctorate must complete another two years and write a thesis. Most study economics, medicine, or law. University teaching is still very traditional, with teachers lecturing to large numbers of students.

Spain has both state-run and private universities, including a National University for Education at Home, where courses are taught via mail, television, and radio. Over 25 percent of university students attend the main universities in Madrid and Barcelona.

Religion

Catholicism is the main religion in Spain. It has played a key role in the history of the country and is still very significant in the lives of the people. The Church's influence can be seen in the art and literature of Spain, in the impressive number of saints, and in the large number of religious congregations and orders. A Catholic marriage is the basis for the family, which, in turn, is considered the foundation of Spanish society.

The Church's influence in Spanish society has declined sharply in recent years, however. Freedom of religion was established by the 1978 constitution, and Catholicism is no longer the official state

Below: **A service is held at the shrine of the Virgin of El Rocío, an important pilgrimage site in Andalusia. Many Catholic Spaniards take part in pilgrimages, known as *romerías* (rom-er-EE-ahs).**

religion. Officially, nevertheless, more than 94 percent of the population is still reported as being Roman Catholic. While not many attend mass regularly, most Spaniards still take part in the traditional church rituals of baptisms, marriages, funerals, and religious festivals such as Christmas and Easter. Women make up the majority of the faithful and are the ones most influenced by religious laws. The Church supported the democratic movement in Spain and so helped foster the new attitude of tolerance and personal freedom found in present-day Spain. A major step for individual liberty came in 1981, when divorce was legalized.

Spain has more than sixty thousand Catholic churches, as well as many monasteries and convents run by different religious orders. Every small town celebrates its saint's day as well as the smallest highlights of the Christian calendar. Even Spaniards who are not strict Roman Catholics get caught up in joyful religious celebrations.

Many of Spain's non-Catholic citizens are members of Protestant churches. Small Eastern Orthodox congregations also exist. Jews form the largest community outside of Christians. A remnant of Moorish conquest and a feature of recent immigration, Islam is also practiced in Spain.

HOLY WEEK

Holy Week is the most important week for Catholic Spaniards. Processions and sermons commemorate the death and resurrection of Jesus Christ. Hundreds of robed and hooded people walk through the streets, some carrying heavy wooden crosses just as Jesus did.
(A Closer Look, page 60)

Left: **Corpus Christi is a religious feast that usually falls at the end of May. It celebrates the triumph of good over evil with a parade through streets carpeted with flowers and scented herbs. Even young children stay up all night to make these carpets.**

Language and Literature

What we today call the Spanish language is actually Castilian. As the kingdom of Castile grew in dominance in the fifteenth century, the dialect of Castile became the accepted language, and Castilian was declared the official language of Spain in 1714. It has a distinctive lisp, with a "th" sound used for the letters S and Z.

Castilian Spanish is a Romance language, meaning one that is descended from Latin, the language of the Roman Empire. While the majority of Spanish words evolved from Latin, some have earlier sources, such as the Greek, Basque, and Celtic languages. Later immigrants also introduced new words. The Visigoths introduced a few Germanic words, the Muslim conquerors introduced Arabic, and some French and Italian also crept into Spanish vocabulary. While the Spanish empire was at its height, words from Native American languages were also absorbed.

Spain also contains three non-Castilian-speaking regions; the people of Galicia, the Basque Country, and Catalonia each have their own language.

Above: **Emphatic gestures add to many conversations.**

THE CONQUEST OF THE AMERICAS

Why do people in Mexico, Peru, and other Latin American countries speak Spanish? Much of Latin America was part of the Spanish empire from the fifteenth to nineteenth century, and Spanish became the official language in Spain's colonies.
(A Closer Look, page 53)

Literature

Given the history and significance of Catholicism in the country, it is not surprising that the majority of Spanish literature is either a religious story or has a religious theme. Perhaps the most famous examples of early literature are the epic poems composed by Spanish minstrels during the Middle Ages. These epics often told of the struggles of Christian kingdoms against the Moors. A surviving example is the anonymous epic poem *The Song of the Cid*, which tells of the trials and triumphs of the Castilian leader known as El Cid.

The most famous work of Spanish literature is the novel *The History of the Valorous and Witty Knight-errant, Don Quixote of the Mancha*, written by Miguel de Cervantes (1547–1616). Lope de Vega (1562–1635) and Pedro Calderón de la Barca (1600–1681) wrote brilliant plays. The 1989 Nobel Prize in Literature was awarded to Spanish novelist Camilo José Cela. Other Spanish Nobel prizewinners were dramatists José Echegaray in 1904 and Jacinto Benavente in 1922, and lyric poets Juan Ramón Jiménez in 1956 and Vicente Aleixandre in 1977. The poet and playwright Federico García Lorca (1898–1936) has also gained international acclaim.

Opposite: **An illustration from *Don Quixote*. Miguel de Cervantes wrote about the comic adventures of Don Quixote and his servant, Sancho Panza, as they traveled the countryside fighting injustice. The story also deals with many serious universal issues and is considered a great work of literature.**

Arts

Architecture

Spain has been exposed to a wide variety of cultural and artistic influences throughout its history. The country has been a melting pot for Muslim and Christian civilization, and its buildings reflect the eight hundred years of Moorish rule, the influence of French, Celtic, and North African settlers, and the importance of Catholicism. Many Spanish buildings are a combination of Eastern and Western design and are suited to the Mediterranean climate. Houses are typically made of brick, are painted white (to reflect the sun), and have wide arches and windows open to the breeze.

The Moors built beautiful mosques and fortified palaces known as *alcazares* (al-kah-THA-res). Among the most famous is the Alhambra in Granada. Spain also has many fine churches. One of the most well known is the unfinished Church of the Sagrada Família in Barcelona. It is the work of Catalan architect Antonio Gaudí (1852–1926). He was obsessed with his church and worked on the project tirelessly until his death.

Below: **The Moors left a stunning architectural legacy in Spain. The Alhambra is one of the most famous palaces in the world.**

PABLO PICASSO

The most famous twentieth-century Spanish artist is the painter and sculptor Pablo Picasso (1881–1973). He pioneered the cubist style and is generally considered the greatest artist of the twentieth century. As well as being a unique inventor of different styles and techniques, he was one of the most prolific artists in history, having created more than twenty thousand works.

(A Closer Look, page 66)

Painting Masters

Three painters stand out from the period before the twentieth century. The first was El Greco (1541–1614). Although born in Crete (Greece), he did most of his work in Spain after moving to Toledo in 1577. He painted his first Spanish commission, the *Assumption of the Virgin,* for the Church of Santo Domingo el Antiguo. His greatest masterpiece, however, is *The Burial of the Count of Orgaz* for the Church of Santo Tomé in Toledo. This work, still in place, portrays a fourteenth-century Toledan nobleman being laid in his grave by Saint Stephen and Saint Augustine.

The second great artist of this early era was the court painter Diego Velázquez (1599–1660). He is known for painting in the style known as realism. In 1623, after painting a portrait of the king, he was named the official painter to King Philip IV.

The third member of this trio is Francisco de Goya (1746–1828). Goya was greatly affected by the horrors of warfare, which he portrayed in his paintings and etchings. In 1814, he completed *Second of May, 1808* and *Third of May, 1808,* which depict the horrifying and dramatically brutal massacres of unarmed Spanish street fighters by French soldiers during Napoleon's occupation.

Twentieth-century artists broke new ground. Joan Miró, Juan Gris, Pablo Picasso, and Salvador Dalí were important Spanish painters who had a strong influence on the art movements of their time. Picasso founded the cubist art movement.

Below: Seated Old Man, 1970/71, by Pablo Picasso.

Salvador Dalí

The twentieth-century surrealist painter Salvador Dalí (1904–1989) portrayed dream imagery and everyday objects in unexpected forms, such as limp watches in *The Persistence of Memory*. Much of his work explored the subconscious. His later paintings, often on religious themes, are more classical in style.

Dance and Music

Modern Spanish dance reflects various influences, including Moorish court entertainment, theatrical dance under Ferdinand and Isabella, and religious dances. Regional dances include the jota of Aragón, the sevillanas of Andalusia, the sardana of Catalonia, and the widespread dances of the bolero and the fandango. Flamenco, the dance of the Gypsies of southern Spain, is world famous.

Spain is also famous for its musicians and composers. With the arrival of Spanish guitar virtuoso Andrés Segovia (1893–1987), the guitar was finally taken seriously as an instrument of classical music. Spaniards Plácido Domingo, José Carreras, and Montserrat Caballé are among the greatest opera singers in the world today.

Above: The Salvador Dalí museum is in Figueras, Catalonia, Dalí's birthplace. Besides painting, Dalí wrote and illustrated books, produced surrealist films, handcrafted jewelry, and created theatrical sets and costumes. His writings include several books, such as *The Secret Life of Salvador Dalí* and the humbly titled *Diary of a Genius.*

Composer Manuel de Falla (1876–1946) is an important name on the Spanish music scene. He strongly felt that a nation's folk songs should be the basis for its music. Generally, however, he did not use actual Spanish folk songs in his work but created themes of his own in the spirit of Spanish folk music. His compositions include *Nights in the Gardens of Spain* for orchestra and piano, the ballet *The Three-Cornered Hat*, and the opera *Life Is Short*. Other notable Spanish composers include Isaac Albéniz (1860–1909) and Enrique Granados (1867–1916).

Left: **The fancy footwork and fluid hand movements of flamenco dancing are accompanied by a guitarist, a singer, a person clapping the rhythm, and the dancers' castanets.**

FLAMENCO

Intricate footwork and graceful hand movements are not enough to make a true flamenco dancer. The dancer must also move the audience with his or her fiery spirit and restrained passion.
(*A Closer Look, page 56*)

Leisure and Festivals

Spaniards have a genuine appreciation of leisure time. After a day's work, many will meet their friends in the village square or at an open-air café for a drink and a chat. On weekends, families like to go outdoors for picnics or take short trips into the countryside to visit relatives. Sunday morning church services are followed by the main Sunday meal at lunchtime. The afternoon is reserved for sports or other activities such as opera or concerts. In the summer months, bullfighting is in season; in winter, soccer is the sport to watch.

Traditionally, a favorite Spanish pastime was to take a stroll in the early evening, then sit and tell stories after dinner. In modern

Below: **A family gathers at a park in Madrid for a picnic followed by a game of cards.**

times, however, these quiet pleasures are often replaced by television. In large cities, much of the fun starts in the evening, and whole families are out in the plazas with friends until late at night. Gambling has also gained in popularity since the mid-1980s, when government-run lotteries started. Casino gambling, betting on soccer games and horse races, bingo, and slot machines are popular throughout Spain. Registered blind persons and handicapped people work for a popular lottery called ONCE. They are a familiar sight on the main street corners of every Spanish town.

Soccer

Soccer is the leading spectator sport in Spain. Major teams such as Real Madrid or FC Barcelona play in enormous stadiums, and more than 100,000 fans turn out each Sunday to watch their team play in the Spanish League, King's Cup, or European competitions. The soccer season runs from September to May, with the top games usually played on Sunday. Spanish teams are among the best in Europe, and their national team is among the best in the world.

Soccer clubs became symbols of regional identity when regional politics were banned under General Francisco Franco, who was in power from 1939 to 1975. For instance, a win by the Basque team, Atletic Bilbao, was regarded as a victory for Basque nationalism. Some of this attitude still persists today and can make matches passionate events.

Soccer has a long history in Spain. It was first played in 1873, when English and Scottish workers at Spanish mines introduced the new game called football. The first club was formed in 1880, and by 1910, most of the clubs still in existence today, including Real Madrid and FC Barcelona, had been formed. Spain joined the international football association (FIFA) in 1904, and the Spanish Football Federation was formed in 1913. Although the game suffered during the Spanish Civil War and World War II, Spain has developed a strong team again.

Above: **The national soccer team played its first game in 1920 and held an excellent record until the outbreak of civil war in 1936. After World War II, the strength of Spain's soccer team began to grow again. Spain has qualified for nine World Cup Finals.**

Outdoor Sports

Golf has become increasingly popular in Spain and is played throughout the year. One of Spain's best-known sportsmen is the talented golfer Severiano Ballesteros. Born in Pedreña in 1957, Ballesteros turned professional at the age of seventeen and won his first major tournament, the British Open, in 1979, becoming the youngest player to do so in the twentieth century. He has gone on to win the British Open twice more and has also won the Masters tournament twice. Spain has also produced world champion-level athletes in tennis and cycling. The fiery tennis phenomenon Arantxa Sánchez Vicario has won four Grand Slam titles, the first being the 1989 French Open (when she was just seventeen years old). She played for Spain in the 1992 and 1996 Olympics. Spaniard Miguel Indurain, a dominant presence on the professional cycling circuit in the 1990s, won the prestigious Tour de France five times in a row, from 1991 to 1995.

Water sports are also extremely popular in Spain, especially at resorts, where adventurous vacationers (and professionals) can water ski, wind surf, sail, and go deep-sea fishing.

JAI ALAI

Jai alai, a ball game invented in Basque, is one of the fastest games in the world. During rapid rallies between players, the ball may travel at a speed of 150 miles (241 km) per hour!
(A Closer Look, page 62)

Below: **Spain's extensive coastline, as well as the Canary and Balearic islands, provide great opportunities for those drawn to wind surfing, sailing, or swimming.**

Left: Arantxa Sánchez Vicario is Spain's tennis champion. Winner of four Grand Slam singles titles, she also won the silver medal for singles and the bronze medal for doubles at the 1996 Olympic Games in Atlanta.

Bullfighting

The bullfight, a longstanding Spanish tradition, has been called a *fiesta brava* (fee-ES-tah BRAH-vah), or a celebration of bravery. Although an increasing number of Spaniards oppose bullfighting on the grounds of its cruelty, the sport remains second only to soccer as the nation's most popular pastime. It is far more than a mere spectator sport; fans applaud not only the bravery of the bullfighters but their dexterity and artistry as well. The bullfight is regarded as the ultimate test of a person's intelligence and will against the formidable strength of the bull, which has been specially bred for its aggressiveness.

Most Spanish cities have at least one bullring. Those in Seville and Madrid are considered the top venues for the sport.

Jai Alai

A distinctive sport is *jai alai* (HYE a-LYE), or *pelota vasca* (peh-LOH-tah VAS-kah). This fast ball game, played in a walled concrete court, is played mainly in the Basque region. *Jai alai* means "merry festival" in the Basque language. The sport probably evolved in the seventeenth century. The *pelota*, Spanish for "ball," is about three-quarters the size of a baseball but much harder and faster.

BULLFIGHTING

Bullfighting is more than just a sport in Spain — it is considered an art. Bullfights are the highlight of many festivals.
(*A Closer Look*, page 46)

Festivals

Central to Spanish life are fiestas, or popular festivals. The creative beauty of the many fiestas held each year comes from the wealth of Spanish traditions and historical influences. Religious festivals are particularly important. These festivals are perhaps as important for strengthening bonds of community and tradition as for being religious ceremonies.

The most important Catholic religious festivals are Holy Week before Easter and Corpus Christi in May. National as well as local celebrations are often held to celebrate a saint's day. These usually begin with a mass, followed by a solemn procession in which religious statues are carried on the shoulders of the participants. Music, dancing, poetry, and singing often enliven these colorful occasions.

Christmas is celebrated on December 25. January 6 is the Feast of the Three Kings. Gifts are exchanged on this day, which commemorates the visit by the three kings of Orient to the baby Jesus, bearing gifts of gold, frankincense, and myrrh.

Carnival celebrations are held all over the country in February, before the beginning of Lent. For many Catholics, this is a chance to dress up and be merry before Lent's sacrifices.

Below: **The Seville Spring Fair, or Feria de Abril, is held every year at Easter. The main event is a horseback parade with men in broad-brimmed hats and women in flamboyant dresses. Bullfights follow later in the day.**

March is the month of Las Fallas in Valencia, when the city is invaded by immense papier mâché sculptures, frequently humorous satires of celebrities. The sculptures are set ablaze on March 19, the feast day of San José (Saint Joseph), much to the delight of revelers.

Holy Week, or Semana Santa, is celebrated in the spring with religious processions of great beauty and tradition. The most original and important processions are in Valladolid, where it is a dour, somber occasion; Cuenca in Castile, where it is celebrated as a sacred music festival; and in Seville where it becomes an almost theatrical showcase of religious fervor.

The Rocío pilgrimage is held in May. This is a traditional Andalusian procession to the Hermitage of the Virgin of the Rocío in Almonte. It has strong southern, even Gypsy, influences as the vast procession of people on horseback and in decorated carts travels to the shrine. The journey involves camping along the way and is as much an occasion for music, dancing, drinking, and horsemanship as it is for religious worship.

Above: **Participants in La Tomatina, an annual fiesta in Buñol, Valencia, throw thousands of tomatoes at each other in a giant food fight.**

RUNNING WITH THE BULLS

The Feast of San Fermin is celebrated every July in Pamplona. While some events are relatively tame, the highlight of the week is the running of the bulls. Each morning, six bulls are released into the streets, and hundreds of people test their own daring and speed running in front of and alongside them.
(A Closer Look, page 68)

Food

Left: **Paella is a popular Valencian rice dish, cooked in a shallow pan. The ingredients may include vegetables, such as tomatoes, peppers, and beans, along with seafood, pork, chicken, or rabbit.**

Regional Cuisines

Spanish cooking is plentiful and varied, like the country itself. The north is one of the richest culinary areas and is well known for its seafood, including cod and hake from the Atlantic Ocean. Basque cooking is world famous, especially its delicious baby eels. In Asturias, the dish to try is *fabada* (fah-BAH-dah), a stew made from beans, sausage, and other meats.

Aragón offers a number of dishes with spicy sauces using red peppers known as *chilindrones* (chil-in-DRON-nes), as well as fine ham made in Teruel. Catalonia is the land of casseroles. Fine sausages, cheeses, and regional sauces are also part of the cuisine, some of them world-famous, such as *ali-oli* (AH-lee OH-lee), made with garlic and olive oil.

Valencia and the surrounding region specialize in rice dishes. The best known is *paella* (pie-AY-yah), which is named after the shallow iron pan in which the rice, seafood, and other items are cooked. Andalusia is the land of fried food, particularly fried fish. Much of its cuisine shows Arab influence. *Gazpacho* (gas-PAH-cho) is a cold soup of vegetables liquefied in a blender. Central Spain is known for its roasts. Lamb, veal, pork, and other meats are slowly roasted in wood ovens.

Drinks and Tapas

Because of the warm climate, most Spanish families eat a lot of fish, fruit, and vegetables. Wine accompanies most meals. A popular drink on hot days is *sangría* (sang-GREE-ya), a mixture of red wine, soda water, fruit, and ice. Coffee, usually served black and strong, is the most popular hot drink.

Tapas (TAH-pahs) are eaten throughout Spain. They are snacks, but are a lot more elaborate than most snack foods. They may include plates of artichokes, cheese, olives, and spicy sausage. More elaborate tapas dishes include mussels in vinaigrette, snails in garlic, and even fried pig ears.

Mealtimes

Breakfast normally consists of coffee or hot chocolate with croissants, toast, or strips of dough called *churros* (CHEW-ros). A midmorning snack is usually eaten around 11 a.m. Families used to return home for lunch, the main meal, while dinner was a lighter, cold meal. This custom is changing, however, with modern work requirements of a continuous workday.

Below: Churros, sugared strips of fried dough, are a favorite with children.

42

A CLOSER LOOK AT SPAIN

Spain is known for its bullfights, flamenco, and Gypsies — for good reason, too. After soccer, bullfighting is the most popular sport in Spain. Nearly every town and village has at least one bullring. An equally daring event is the running of the bulls every July in Pamplona. Flamenco dance, less dangerous, but still well-loved, is popular throughout Spain. It was originally performed by Gypsies, a group of people living in Spain since the 1400s.

Below: **A procession of decorated carts winds its way to the Hermitage of the Virgin of the Rocío during an annual pilgrimage to this shrine to the Virgin Mary.**

The country is steeped in tradition. Catholicism has been identified with Spain since the sixth century, and today it is still an integral part of Spanish culture. Spain is also famous for its distinctive regional traditions, such as the winemaking of La Rioja and the language and folklore of the Basque Country.

Spain's influence has been felt far beyond its borders — Christopher Columbus's voyages in the fifteenth century opened up the Americas to settlement by the Spanish. This section will explore the heyday of the Spanish empire and how its legacy in the South American continent remains strong today.

Opposite: **Toledo has a long and rich history, dating back to the Roman Empire. The historic city center includes many old buildings and narrow, cobbled streets.**

The Basque Region

Basques, the most ancient surviving ethnic group in Western Europe, settled along the coast of the Bay of Biscay in Roman times. They live in an area stretching from Bilbao in Spain to Bayonne in France. Most Basques in Spain live in the Basque Country. The Basque language, Euskara, is unrelated to any other European language and is one of the most distinct features of their culture. Most Basques also speak Spanish or French.

Traditionally, Basques were farmers, shipbuilders, and seafarers. Today, Pais Vasco, as the Basque region is also called, is a major manufacturing area. In addition to the lumber and furniture industries, Bilbao has steel mills that provide a large portion of the iron and steel produced in the country.

Left: **Many Basques living along the coast became expert shipbuilders and seafarers. As early as the fourteenth and fifteenth centuries, Basques were venturing as far as Greenland and Newfoundland on whaling and fishing expeditions. Fish is still an important part of their cuisine today.**

During the early twentieth century, the Basques' desire to manage their own affairs led to considerable conflict in Spain. In 1936, during the Spanish Civil War, an independent Basque republic was proclaimed. In 1937, however, General Franco bombed Guernica, a town of symbolic importance to the Basques. The Basque government was forced to go into exile. Many Basques left for the Americas, while their national government fled to Paris.

After the death of General Franco in 1975, the separatist movement intensified. The new 1978 Spanish constitution allowed the Basques limited independence, including their own parliament, police force, and tax system. Despite these concessions, the terrorist-liberation organization ETA (Basque Homeland and Freedom) has been responsible for more than eight hundred deaths.

Some Basque extremists claim they are a different ethnic group from the rest of Spain and, therefore, deserve their own country. To most people, however, the only difference is the Basque language. Although the Spanish government has granted greater autonomy to Spain's Basques and other ethnic groups, the Basques' demands continue to be one of the main problems facing the government today.

Above: **There is a strong separatist movement among the Basques. The most militant of them demand secession from Spain.**

Bullfighting

Bullfighting is undoubtedly the most famous Spanish spectacle. After soccer, it is the country's favorite sport, although it has been losing popularity over the years as more people consider it cruel. The bulls bred in Spain are known to be aggressive, and, as long ago as 228 B.C., they were used in battle to help defeat Spain's enemies. The tradition of bullfighting developed as a way for men to prove their strength and courage by challenging one of these ferocious animals.

Most of the fights take place in a round arena. The audience sits in tiers around a central ring. The fight begins with a grand procession of matadors (the bullfighters), their assistants, and local government representatives. Each matador is dressed in a short jacket, vest, and knee-length, skintight trousers of silk and satin. The outfit is richly embroidered in gold and silver. For the opening ceremony, the matador also wears a large dress cape and a wide-brimmed hat called a *montera* (mon-TEH-rah).

Below: **The final test of strength and speed in a bullfight is between the bull and matador alone.**

Left: **Posters advertise upcoming bullfights. The bullrings in Seville and Madrid are considered the main arenas for bullfights.**

The procession crosses the arena; then, a local official, usually the mayor, throws down the key to the bull pen. The matador gets ready as one of his assistants releases the bull.

The Fight Begins

The matador's main weapons are his sword and a red cape that he waves to encourage the bull to attack. The fight begins when the matador performs the first sweeps of his cape. A bugle sounds, and an assistant appears on horseback. He gallops around, teasing the bull. Fending off the bull's charges with a long pole, he turns it back toward the matador. The horses wear protective armor to prevent being stabbed by the bull's horns.

At a second bugle call, another team of assistants, this time on foot, runs into the ring. They carry long sticks with sharp spikes at the end, which they jab at the bull's neck when it charges. This is to weaken the bull's neck muscles so its head hangs low enough at the end of the fight for the matador to be able to kill it with his sword.

The Hour of Truth

A third bugle signals it is time for the killing, also known as the Hour of Truth. The matador now faces the bull alone. After proving his skills by performing many dangerous and graceful passes with his cape, he thrusts his sword into the bull's neck in a move that, if performed correctly, causes almost instant death. The following day, the bull is taken to a local butcher.

The Changing Role of Women

Above: **Many Spanish women pursue higher degrees in universities.**

Among many of the changes that have taken place in Spanish society in recent years, the role of women stands out. Spanish women have traditionally stayed home to look after the family. They cooked, kept house, and raised the children. This role has been reinforced by the strong influence of the Catholic Church. Some women, however, are beginning to make other choices and are pursuing careers. Despite church opposition, divorce is now legal. Abortion is legal for health reasons.

Under the rule of General Francisco Franco, Spanish women had to get a certificate of their husbands' approval before they could take a job. Today, more and more married women have jobs. Girls and single women were once kept under strict family control until they were married; now, young people can mix freely.

New Opportunities

Changes for women began in the 1960s, along with the growing women's movement in many Western countries. Two main factors led to this change. The first was increasing migration from rural areas to the cities. This removed women from their traditional communities, where rigid social rules were still in place. The move also opened up more job opportunities.

Second, the level of education for women has improved. Women used to leave school early to concentrate on domestic duties but now reach the same average education levels as men. This trend began when school attendance until the age of fourteen was made compulsory for all Spaniards. Since then, the number of women enrolled in secondary and higher education has increased dramatically. Over the last five years, the percentage of women in higher education increased by 40 percent.

As women have gained greater levels of education and taken jobs outside the home, their status has risen in society, and the choices available to them have grown. The proportion of women in the job force has risen from 20 percent in 1950 to over 38 percent in 1997. This statistic does not mean that Spanish women are completely emancipated, however. In fact, traditional roles and male machismo are still reinforced by religious and social values.

Below: **This woman works in the Prado Museum in Madrid. She is restoring a painting by the Italian artist Sandro Botticelli.**

Christopher Columbus

Christopher Columbus is famous for sailing to the New World, now known as North America and South America. He is remembered as one of the greatest mariners, or seamen, of all time.

Columbus was born in Genoa, Italy, in 1451. His sense of adventure and a love of the sea saw him set sail for England in 1476. Legend has it that pirates attacked his fleet off the coast of Portugal. Although the ship sank, Columbus managed to swim to shore and made his way to Lisbon, the capital of Portugal.

This was a period in history when attention was focused on finding a shorter sea route from Europe to Asia. Columbus believed that Asia could be reached faster by sailing west rather

Below: **Columbus went to King Ferdinand and Queen Isabella of Spain with his proposal to seek a western sea route to Asia. He was granted an audience in 1486, but it was not until 1492 that an agreement was finally reached between the monarchs and Columbus.**

than east around the southern tip of Africa. In 1484, he asked John II, king of Portugal, to finance an exploratory journey west across the Atlantic Ocean. His proposal was rejected because Portuguese ships were already sailing around Africa.

Seeking royal backing for his plan, Columbus moved to Spain, where King Ferdinand and Queen Isabella agreed to sponsor the expedition. He set sail from Spain on August 3, 1492.

Sailing the Ocean Blue

The sailing party consisted of three vessels, the *Niña*, the *Pinta*, and the *Santa María*. Land was sighted after a treacherous voyage of over two months, and on October 12, 1492, the expedition landed on Guanahani, an island in the Bahamas. Columbus told the natives that, by right of conquest, their island now belonged to Spain. He renamed it *San Salvador*, meaning "Holy Savior." During the next few weeks, he also landed on Cuba and the island of Hispaniola. Columbus returned to Spain triumphant and was made the official viceroy of this new territory known as the West Indies. Until the day he died, he believed that he had reached his goal of sailing to Asia. Although Columbus was mistaken, he still ranks as a great explorer. Few other navigators of his time would have dared to sail westward into the great unknown.

Left: Columbus greets a Cuban chief. The arrival of Columbus's ships in the Western Hemisphere was one of the pivotal events in world history. It opened up the so-called "New World" to European colonization and initiated the spread of Western civilization to a new hemisphere. Columbus's arrival was catastrophic for native Americans, however. Over the years, many were driven off their lands, killed, or died of diseases.

The Conquest of the Americas

The discovery of the New World in 1492 led to the expansion of the Spanish empire into the Western Hemisphere. The American continents contained all the natural wealth for which people longed — and far more. Great deposits of gold and vast reserves of other minerals lay untapped. Mile upon mile of plains, valleys, and mountains offered fertile farmland and pastures.

The earliest settlements were in the West Indies. Hispaniola had the first towns. Santo Domingo, established in 1496, became the first capital of New Spain. Other settlements appeared in Cuba, Puerto Rico, and Jamaica. Explorers led expeditions along the coasts and into the heart of the American continents.

Although the territories in the Western Hemisphere were new to these Spaniards, cultures dating back twenty thousand years already existed. Some civilizations, such as the Aztecs and Incas, were highly advanced, settled agricultural communities with central cities and imposing monuments. These native cultures were all but wiped out by the new settlers. Hernán Cortés conquered the empire of the Aztecs in Mexico between 1519 and 1521. A few years later, in 1532, the gold-seeking Francisco Pizarro reached Peru, land of the Incas. The fall of the Inca empire to Pizarro and his handful of men is considered one of the tragedies of history. The spirit of the people was broken after a few disastrous rebellions.

The Spanish empire flourished through such conquests. Gold and silver poured into the Spanish king's treasury, rousing the envy of other rulers. Portugal, France, and Great Britain all fought for control of New World territories, and established colonies that lasted over two hundred years. Most of these became independent from Europe between 1775 and 1825. Cuba and Puerto Rico did not become free of Spain until 1898.

Spain still has a lot in common with its former colonies. The Spanish spoken in Mexico, Peru, Cuba, Puerto Rico, and other Latin American countries is the Castilian language. Catholicism, brought over by Spanish missionaries, remains the main religion. These cultural ties have allowed Spain to maintain strong political ties with the region; friendship and cooperation treaties have been signed with Argentina, Mexico, Venezuela, Chile, and Brazil.

Above: **The majority of the population in Mexico is mestizo — of mixed Spanish and native American blood. Spain left behind a pervasive legacy in its former colonies. Many Latin Americans are mestizos. Spanish is the official language, and Roman Catholicism, introduced by missionaries, remains the main religion.**

Opposite: **A Spanish priest addresses the Inca leader, Atahuallpa. When Spanish explorer Francisco Pizarro arrived in Peru, the Inca empire stretched from the Pacific coast across the Andes to the Atlantic and from Ecuador southward to central Chile.**

Doñana National Park

Treasured Wetlands

Doñana National Park, in the province of Andalusia, adjoins the estuary of the Guadalquivir River where it meets the Atlantic Ocean. Covering a core area of 125,329 acres (50,720 hectares), and with a further 133,928 acres (54,200 hectares) of surrounding area also protected, the Doñana wetlands have been designated a World Heritage Property by the United Nations.

The lagoons, marshlands, and coastal sand dunes of this national park are highly valued because of the diversity of plants and animals they sustain. Every year, thousands of birds — approximately one hundred and fifty species — pass through Doñana, which is the main stopping place on their migration between Europe and Africa. Flocks of up to seventy thousand greylag geese and two hundred thousand teal can be seen. In spring, spoonbills come to nest. Herons and flamingos are a common sight, and even some red kites and short-toed eagles have been spotted.

Above: **The wetlands of Doñana became officially protected in 1969. The marshes flood in winter after the summer drought is over and provide an ideal winter stopover for many birds.**

Endangered Species

Doñana is a refuge for many endangered species, including the Spanish lynx. Other animals, such as wild boars, fallow deer, red deer, foxes, and otters, are common. Seventeen reptile, nine amphibian, and eight fish species are also registered as breeding in the park. Many environmental research projects are carried out there. To avoid harm to the fragile environment, the number of visitors is controlled, and a local guide must accompany them.

Tragic Toxic Spill

Doñana suffered a serious disaster in April 1998, when a toxic spill from a mine near Seville contaminated Guadiamar River, which flows through the park. Thousands of dead fish floated to the surface of the river, corpses of birds were scattered along the banks, and vast areas of crops in nearby farmland were ruined. Engineers quickly set up makeshift dikes along the riverbanks to try to keep the toxic sludge away from the national park. Volunteers tried to prevent birds from eating the fish, frogs, crabs, and other creatures that had died of the river toxins, by clearing the carcasses and scaring birds away. To some extent, these efforts appear to have worked, but the true damage can only be assessed over time.

Left: **About sixty pairs of lynx live in Doñana National Park. They are one of the world's rarest mammals.**

Flamenco

The flamenco is the most famous Spanish dance and song form. It is essentially about passion; expressing this emotion is more important than the singer having a beautiful voice or the dancer performing intricate steps. What is essential is that the dance and song come from deep inside the performer and convey the emotions of the lyrics.

Although now a national dance, flamenco was originally a local style. Traditionally performed by the Gypsies of Andalusia, the dance has developed over many centuries from Gypsy, Moorish, Andalusian, and other influences. It became known as flamenco in the early nineteenth century after the music and dance style became popular in café entertainment.

Flamenco songs, or *cante* (KAHN-teh), have three different styles. The first style is very grand and full of depth. Songs are intense and moving, tragic in tone, and full of emotion. The second style is moderately serious, the music having a quick rhythm and sometimes sounding almost Asian. The third form is light and exuberant, with lyrics about love and nature. Latin American influence has also appeared in some genres of song, such as the *rumbas gitanas* (ROOM-bahs hee-TAHN-ahs) and the *colombianas* (koh-lom-bee-YAH-nahs). The main flamenco dance, called the grand dance, is believed to still have elements of classical Indian dance that reflect the Gypsies' origins in India.

Individual singers and dancers add improvised music, words, and moves to create a unique style of their own. In general, male dancers' steps include intricate toe and heel clicking, while the traditional women's dance concentrates on fluid body and hand movements. Both dancers seek to express the emotions of the flamenco songs.

The use of castanets in flamenco has become more common over the years, an accompaniment that has been picked up from Andalusian dance. Today, it is also common for accompanying guitarists to be part of the flamenco experience. Guitarists may also perform solos. The audience is expected to participate by shouting and clapping along with the dancers. Increasing interest in large public performances has meant that routines are now much more carefully rehearsed rather than spontaneously created on stage.

Above: **Young Spaniards learn flamenco dance steps.**

Opposite: **A proud and elegant posture is very important in flamenco. The audience often helps the dancer and the musicians keep the rhythm by snapping or clapping to the beat of the music.**

Gypsies

Gypsies are believed to have arrived in Spain by the fifteenth century. Most are nomadic, meaning they roam around the country rather than settle in one particular place. The majority live around Madrid, Barcelona, and other large cities in southern Spain, where the climate is more temperate and suited to an outdoor way of life.

Modern historians have concluded that the Gypsies first came from the Punjab in northwestern India. About one thousand years ago, these people fled to escape fierce fighting between Arab and Mongolian invaders. During their journey west, many settled in the Middle East, Persia, and Egypt. In fact, they became so closely associated with Egypt that they eventually started to believe they were descendants of the old kings, or pharaohs. This legend is still referred to in many of their songs and explains how they got their name. Gypsies used to call themselves "Egyptians," or "Gypcians," and this eventually was shortened to Gypsies.

Gypsies originally spoke a language called Romany (which has been identified by linguists as a simplified version of Sanskrit), but today's Spanish Gypsies speak mostly Castilian. Traditionally, they made their living as tinkers (metalsmiths or pot repairers), menders of the woven backs and seats of old chairs, wandering musicians,

Above: **Nomadic Gypsies usually travel in caravans of cars, trailers, or wagons. Not all Gypsies are nomadic, however, and many have been absorbed into the mainstream of Spanish life. They have created their own political organizations, and some have been elected to the Spanish parliament.**

fortune-tellers, or by begging and stealing. This earned them a bad reputation that has persisted, even though most modern Gypsies are honest, hard-working people.

Gypsy society is based on an old class system, which, to some extent, still operates today. While some attempts have been made to integrate them with the rest of Spanish society, Gypsies have tried to keep their own culture and traditions alive. They tend to live apart and keep to themselves. Poor living conditions are common, and it is difficult for them to gain access to welfare services, such as housing, education, employment, health care, and social services. In 1988, the Ministry of Social Affairs launched the Gypsy Development Program, which aims at full enrollment of school-aged Gypsy children, reduction of unemployment, better health care, and standard housing. It is the first official attempt to fully integrate Gypsies into Spanish society. While it is considered a good idea to help Gypsies make their way in an increasingly modern world, the government has also pledged to help preserve their culture.

Below: Gypsy women have traditionally earned a living through fortune-telling or as entertainers.

Holy Week

For Catholic Spaniards, Holy Week is the most important week of the year. It is the week before Easter and starts with Palm Sunday. Solemn rites commemorate the passion, death, and resurrection of Jesus Christ. Special observances in remembrance of the Eucharist are held on Maundy Thursday; scripture readings, solemn prayers, and veneration of the cross recall the crucifixion of Christ on Good Friday. Holy Saturday commemorates the burial of Christ, and midnight vigil services inaugurate the Easter celebration of the resurrection.

Different towns have their own distinctive celebrations. For example, in old Castilian towns like Burgos and Valladolid, Holy Week is a very serious festival, but in Cuenca it has become a sacred music festival. The largest and most colorful celebrations are held in Seville. Processions include the highly revered images of Virgen de la Macarena, an image of the Virgin Mary whose face is streaked with crystal tears, and Jesus of the Great Power. These statues take their names from the churches where they reside.

Below: **Holy Week processions often include a religious statue of Jesus or the Virgin Mary.**

60

Left: **An outdoor sermon is held in western Castile-León during Holy Week.**

In every case, the week begins with the blessing of palms on Palm Sunday, progresses through the climax of grief, and emerges in triumphant joy the following Sunday. Throughout the week, activity is focused on church services and street processions. Huge floats called *pasos* (PAH-sohs), decorated with flowers and candles and bearing life-size statues, reenact the events of the first Holy Week. The floats are carried by members of various town brotherhoods, who often pay for the privilege of carrying the floats on their shoulders. Others walk as penitents, asking forgiveness of their sins. They may dress in the pointed hoods and robes of the Spanish Inquisition, and some walk barefoot carrying large wooden crosses, as Jesus did on his way to be crucified. The prevailing atmosphere, however, is not miserable. Older people talk at length about the techniques of carrying pasos and the skill of the footwork involved. Sometimes gypsies in the crowd start singing emotional flamenco songs.

Like many other festivals, bullfights also take place during Holy Week. The adult bulls fight in the most important rings and the younger ones in the minor rings of the town.

Jai Alai

Jai alai is a Basque ball game. It spread to Latin America in the late nineteenth century and became a national pastime in many countries. In the early twentieth century, the game was adopted in the United States. Today, the game is played by professionals in Florida, Connecticut, and Rhode Island. Jai alai is also played professionally in southern France, Italy, Mexico, Argentina, Indonesia, and the Philippines.

Jai alai is a type of handball played on a large court. Opposing individuals or teams alternately bounce a small, hard

Above: **A poster advertises a jai alai match in the Basque region.**

Left: **The three-sided court is the most common for jai alai games. Baskets worn by the players can vary greatly from curved to flat, long to short, and leather-lined to rubber-lined.**

ball against one, two, or three walls and catch it upon its return. It is one of the fastest of all games and requires great agility and coordination. The objective of the game is to score points by forcing the opponent to miss the ball, hold it, or throw it out of bounds. The court, known as a *fronton* (fron-TOHN), is a rectangle with solid walls on three sides and a wire screen on the fourth side. Spectators watch from behind the screen.

The *pelota* (peh-LOH-tah), or ball, is three-quarters the size of a baseball and much harder. It is caught and thrown with a glove-shaped wicker basket, which is strapped to the player's wrist.

The speed of play and the hardness of the pelota make jai alai a dangerous game. During fast rallies, the ball can travel more than 150 miles (241 km) per hour. The fastest recorded jai alai ball in the *Guinness Book of Records* is 188 miles (302 km) per hour.

The game starts when a player bounces the pelota and throws it against the front wall. The pelota must land inside two red lines painted across the court. If not, the server loses the point. If it is a successful serve, the ball must be caught in the air or after the first bounce and thrown back against the front wall in one smooth move. If the ball is held, or juggled first in the basket, the team loses the point. If the ball lands out of bounds, the team that threw it loses the point. A rally lasts until the pelota goes out of bounds,

gets dropped, or bounces twice. Either team can score in every rally; they do not have to be serving. Jai alai is played in singles or in doubles. In Europe, a straight singles or doubles game is played with the winner being the first to reach ten or forty points. In the United States, jai alai is mostly played as a singles or doubles round-robin competition. There are normally eight teams, and the first team to get seven points wins.

Jai alai has also been played as an Olympic sport, first in 1924, and most recently in 1992 in Barcelona, where the Spanish team defeated the French team for the gold medal.

Above: Jai alai was introduced to the United States in 1926, with the first professional game being played at a fronton, or court, in Miami, Florida. Today, the game is very popular in the state, and Florida has more jai alai frontons than anywhere else in the world.

La Rioja and Winemaking

La Rioja is famous for its wines. It is an attractive region of unspoiled mountainous country and wide, fertile valleys in north-central Spain. The people of the area live mainly on irrigated farmland along the Ebro River and its tributaries, growing grapes, grain, and other produce. The region receives plenty of rain and has long springs and autumns. The countryside is beautiful, with tall poplars and eucalyptus trees lining the roads and vineyards that cover the hill slopes.

Logroño, the regional capital, is the trading and industrial center for this rich agricultural region. Other industries include food processing and the manufacture of textiles, furniture, chemicals, and perfumes. Founded in pre-Roman times, the city was annexed to the former kingdom of Castile in 1173. Logroño today includes an ancient part of town and a modern district.

There are at present 258 wineries in La Rioja. The chief wine center is Haro. This small town is surrounded by vineyards and thirteen large bodegas, or wine cellars. Clay soils and a climate sheltered by mountains to the north create conditions suitable for

Above: **Unlike central and southern Spain, which have endless dry summers, La Rioja gets plenty of rain and has become one of the most important wine manufacturing regions in the world.**

growing grapes. Life in Haro revolves almost exclusively around this activity, and residents happily douse one another with wine on their major feast day, aptly known as "the battle of the wine."

Harvesting the Grapes

The grape harvest is an important time of the year, and even children get involved. They help first in picking the grapes off the vines, then crushing them in huge barrels with their bare feet. The juice is later fermented to make wine.

Various popular festivals are held throughout the region to celebrate winemaking. The Vendimia Riojana Festival is held in Logroño during the third week of September to celebrate the grape harvest. Festivities include bullfights and a parade of carts.

Aging Wines

La Rioja is best known for its red wines. These wines are left to age in barrels made from oak, which gives them a strong, vanilla-like flavor. Tastings are not as common as in France or the Napa Valley in California, but some of the bodegas near Haro have frequent visitors. Some of the best bodegas were actually founded by immigrants from Bordeaux, France, a well-known wine area.

Below: One of the most popular Rioja wines is red. Grapes are harvested in late summer.

Pablo Picasso

Pablo Picasso (1881–1973), a Spanish painter and sculptor, is considered one of the greatest artists of the twentieth century. He created more than twenty thousand works in his lifetime.

Picasso was born in Málaga on October 25, 1881. He was only ten years old when he painted his first works of art. At the age of fourteen, he performed brilliantly on the entrance examinations to Barcelona's School of Fine Arts. Later, in Madrid, he joined the well-known Academy of San Fernando. Frequent visits to the Prado Museum also shaped his artistic vision.

Picasso first visited Paris, France, in October 1901. Paris was, at the time, the most significant center for all artists. Although he continued traveling between the two countries, by 1904, Picasso had relocated to Paris. He loved the city's street life and painted many pictures of people in dance halls and cafés. During his Blue Period, he painted primarily in blue. During his later Rose Period, he used warmer tones and livelier subjects.

Picasso's maturing work showed the influence of Greek, Iberian, and African art. His 1907 painting *Les Demoiselles d'Avignon* was radical for the times, with its images broken apart

Above: **Pablo Picasso is considered the most influential artist of the twentieth century. He was full of vitality throughout his life and was still painting in his eighties.**

Left: Course de Taureaux, **1934.**

to resemble fractured glass. This style was later described by a critic as lots of "little cubes," and became known as cubism. Picasso continued painting in this style until 1925.

Faces in many of Picasso's cubist paintings, such as *Tête de Femme*, show his interest in African masks. Later paintings, such as *The Pipes of Pan* (1923), were also inspired by mythology. In 1935, Picasso sketched *Minotauromachy*, a picture that shows his fascination with minotaurs and bullfights.

Above: Guernica, **1937. This painting depicts the horror Picasso felt when Guernica, an important town in the Basque region, was bombed during the Spanish Civil War. The painting has now become an important national symbol and is kept in the Prado Museum in Madrid.**

Picasso painted his famous mural *Guernica* after General Francisco Franco asked German planes to bomb the Basque town of Guernica. The raid took place on April 26, 1937, during the Spanish Civil War. The painting is not of the actual bombing, but Picasso showed his outrage by using symbols such as a dying horse, a dead warrior, a mother and dead child, and a woman trapped in a burning building.

During his lifetime, Picasso's style continued to evolve. His interest in surrealism grew in the 1930s, as he increasingly painted emotionally charged subjects. He also produced pottery, among many sculptures and lithographs. His lithograph *Dove* was adopted as the symbol of the World Peace Congress in 1949.

Picasso was one of those few artists whose work is recognized during their lifetime. One of his most significant exhibitions was held in 1971 at the Louvre Museum in Paris, honoring him on his ninetieth birthday. It was the first time a living artist's work had been exhibited at the museum. Picasso died on April 8, 1973.

Running with the Bulls

Pamplona, the capital city of Navarra, is today best known for the annual running of the bulls, which draws tourists from all over the world. Every July, the city celebrates the feast of San Fermin, the town's patron saint, by releasing bulls to run through the streets to the bullring. Bullfights, jai alai matches, fireworks, and singing contests are all part of the festival. From midday on July 6 until midnight on July 14, the city gives itself up to riotous, nonstop celebration.

Fools or Heroes?

Six bulls are released each morning of the nine-day festival to run from their corral near the Plaza San Domingo, through the narrow streets, to Pamplona's bullfighting arena. In front, around, and occasionally under them, run hundreds of locals and tourists who are foolish or brave enough to test their daring against the horns. Beginners often pose as great a danger to experienced runners as to themselves, but anyone can choose to take part. Loudspeakers provide instructions in several languages, but the frenzied panic of the run often leaves little time to remember such instructions. Unlike many bullfights, the animals clearly have the upper hand in this situation. Despite the risks, however, there were only thirteen fatalities between 1924 and 1997.

With the whole town out to cheer them on, the runners, dressed in white and red, first sing a hymn for San Fermin. As the starting rocket goes off, the bulls are released from their pens. The runners take off ahead of them and are soon seen squeezing under or leaping over the barricades into the crowds of spectators or climbing lampposts to escape the horns of the racing bulls. The bulls are rushed along to the bullrings, and the afternoon is taken up with bullfights.

The tradition of running the bulls began in 1591 when a handful of daredevils decided to run through the streets along with bulls being transferred from their corral to the city's bullring. The fiesta has grown steadily since that time. American author Ernest Hemingway's novel *The Sun Also Rises* made this festival world famous, and the area in front of the Plaza de Toros has been renamed Plaza Hemingway by a grateful council.

Opposite: **Each year, thousands of people come for the bull running fiesta of San Fermin in Pamplona. Many risk life and limb to race the bulls. The event is divided into two parts — first the bulls run through the streets to the bullring; next, young bulls with padded horns are let loose among the crowd in the bullring.**

Below: **Bull running in other towns is an equally thrilling event.**

The Spanish Armada

The Spanish Armada was the fleet of ships that King Philip II of Spain sent to invade and conquer England in 1588. The Armada's defeat by the British navy helped establish the supremacy of British power and marked the beginning of the Spanish empire's decline.

Philip II, a fervent Catholic, wanted to attack England for many reasons, some being religious. Mary Stuart, the Catholic queen of Scotland and a potential heir to the English throne, had been executed, and Philip II felt it was his duty as a Catholic to wage war against the English Protestants. Pope Sixtus V promised to give money to Philip II to fight a holy war. Another reason for war was that English pirates had been capturing Spanish ships carrying treasure from the New World and from Africa. A lot of

Left: **Philip II succeeded to the throne after Charles I and reigned from 1556 to 1598. He saw himself as defender of the Roman Catholic Church and believed that the authority of the Church could only be saved by intervening in Protestant England and France. Although the Spanish Armada was defeated, the Spanish empire reached its greatest extent and power during Philip II's rule.**

these stolen goods had found their way into England's royal treasury. The final straw was Queen Elizabeth's knighting of Englishman Francis Drake, who had been trading illegally in Spain's New World territories and pirating Spanish ships.

In May 1588, the supposedly invincible Spanish Armada set sail. Combat between the Spanish and English fleets began on July 21, 1588, in English waters. The English ships were clearly superior to the Spanish fleet. They were faster, easier to navigate, and had longer-range weapons. The Spanish fought by ramming enemy ships and then boarding them and were not prepared for the English tactics of long-range firing. In every encounter, the Armada lost ships. The Spanish fleet retreated to the port of Calais, but the English navy followed, and at midnight on July 28, it sent six booby-trapped ships into Calais harbor. When these boats burst into flames, the Spanish ships cut their anchors free and tried to flee. As the Spanish ships drifted, the British navy attacked. The Armada fled north, where treacherous weather caused many ships to sink or run aground. The Spanish fleet was destroyed.

The defeat of the Armada did not end the war between England and Spain. It spurred the English on, however, and was the first real proof that England now ruled the waves.

Above: **The Spanish Armada had 130 ships, not more than 50 of them real men-of-war, or warships. The English fleet had 197 ships; many were small coastal vessels. The defeat of the Spanish Armada by the English fleet was unexpected and disastrous, and Spain nearly went bankrupt.**

Territories in Africa

Spain has control over Ceuta and Melilla, two small enclaves in Morocco. Both territories played key roles at the start of the Spanish Civil War. A revolt of army officers in the Melilla garrison in 1936 was a prelude to the war. Once the war began, General Francisco Franco dispatched an expedition force from Ceuta to fight in Spain. In 1995, Spain decided to give the two territories the status of autonomous community. This has resulted in strained relations with Morocco, which wants to take control of the cities.

Ceuta

Ceuta is a seaport near the Strait of Gibraltar. The city is governed as part of Cádiz province in Spain. It is on a headland with seven peaks at the end of a narrow isthmus. The highest of these peaks, Mt. Hatcho, is one of the two Pillars of Hercules, as named by the Greeks.

Ceuta has passed through many hands. Early colonization by the Carthaginians and the Romans was followed by the Vandals,

Left: Ceuta is a military post and a free port. It has impressive monuments, such as the rebuilt cathedral from the fifteenth century, the fortress of Mt. Hatcho, and the Church of San Francisco. Today, the town covers an area of 8 square miles (20.7 square km) and has a population of 73,500.

the Byzantine Empire, the Visigoths, and the Arabs. The latter called it Sebta, from which the modern name is derived.

Ceuta became an important center for the manufacture of brassware and for trade in slaves, gold, and ivory under later Berber rulers and Spain's Moorish rulers. The Portuguese captured the city in 1415 and the Spaniards in 1580. Despite many sieges by the Moors, including one that lasted from 1694 to 1720, Ceuta has been a Spanish territory ever since.

Melilla

The other Spanish enclave and port in Africa is Melilla. It is also on the Mediterranean coast and is administered as part of Spain's Málaga province. Founded by the Phoenicians, the settlement was later ruled by the Carthaginians, the Romans, the Byzantine Empire, and various Berber dynasties before being conquered by Spain in 1497. The city exports mineral ores (mainly iron, lead, and zinc), as well as fish and fruit, and has industries such as fish processing, boat building, and wood and flour milling. It serves as a rail terminus for the inland region. The old, walled town is surrounded by modern buildings to the south and west.

Above: Like Ceuta, Melilla has remained Spanish despite a long history of attack and sieges. Today, Melilla covers an area of 4.6 square miles (11.9 square km) and has a population of 63,600.

RELATIONS WITH NORTH AMERICA

Spain, the United States, and Canada are close trading partners today, despite various periods of conflict, and all are members of NATO. Spain and the United States have historical ties that date back to Columbus's arrival in the New World in 1492. A large part of what is now the United States was colonized by Spanish explorers and settlers. In 1779, Spain sided with the colonies against Britain in the American Revolution.

Rivalry between the United States and Spain for influence in the Americas eventually led to the Spanish–American War in

Opposite: **Pedro Menéndez de Avilés was a Spanish sailor who founded St. Augustine, Florida, in 1565. He also explored the Atlantic coast and established a string of forts along the coast.**

1898, which soured relations for many years. In the Spanish Civil War, however, many Americans volunteered on the side of the Republicans. Nationalist victory brought initial condemnation of General Franco and his dictatorial regime by the United States, although friendly relations were still maintained. Diplomatic ties improved greatly when King Juan Carlos took power in 1975.

Above: **In 1786, Spanish Franciscan missionaries in California founded the Santa Barbara Mission — now known as the "Queen of the Missions" because of its lovely architecture.**

Spanish Explorers in North America

By the sixteenth century, the Spanish had established a strong foothold in Central and South America. But they did not know much about the lands farther north, which the local Indians rumored to be richer than both Mexico or Peru. In search of these treasures, Hernando de Soto led a thousand men from Spain to Florida in 1539. They marched through Georgia and Tennessee, crossing the Mississippi River in the spring of 1541. Instead of treasure, however, all they encountered were American Indians. After three more years of searching, de Soto fell ill and died.

Left: **Hernando de Soto's parents wanted him to be a lawyer. His desire for adventure was stronger, however, and in his teens, he set off for the New World. He was part of Francisco Pizarro's famous expedition to Peru and later led his own explorations of North America.**

Francisco Vásquez de Coronado, a Spanish governor in western Mexico, led another long journey to the southwestern United States in 1540. Coronado had heard stories of the Seven Cities of Gold and sent out scouting parties from New Mexico. One came upon the Grand Canyon. Another found Indian pueblos in a fertile area of the Rio Grande Valley. They also found the mouth of the Colorado River in Arizona. None found any gold. Although Coronado returned to Mexico without the treasures he hoped for, he established Spain's later claim to land that now covers a huge portion of the United States — from present-day California to Oklahoma and Kansas.

Above: **The first European sighting of the magnificent Grand Canyon was by the Coronado expedition through Arizona.**

Other Spanish explorers also reached areas that are today part of the United States. In 1565, the city of St. Augustine was founded to protect Spain's vital sea-lane off the Florida coast. In 1598, Spanish pioneers established towns on the Rio Grande headwaters in the present state of New Mexico. San Diego, Los Angeles, and Monterey in California were all founded by the Spanish soldier and explorer Gaspar de Portolá.

Spain's North American territories became part of Mexico when Mexico gained independence. The United States acquired much of its current territory through the 1848 Treaty of Guadalupe Hidalgo with Mexico and the 1853 Gadsden Purchase.

Spanish Missions

While Spain's explorers claimed land and treasure for their country, its priests worked among the native peoples to spread Christianity. The cross of Roman Catholicism was raised at countless missions throughout the far-flung Spanish empire. Spanish attitudes, values, and ideals were spread along with religion in a potent mix that still remains strong five centuries later. Missions were founded in California, New Mexico, Arizona, and Texas.

Junípero Serra, a Franciscan priest, joined the 1769 Spanish expedition to Upper California led by Gaspar de Portolá. Serra founded many missions throughout the present state of California, with the first being Mission San Diego. De Portolá named San Francisco for the Spanish Franciscan monks. These missions helped strengthen Spain's control in California.

Spanish Influence Today

Spain's historical influence is very evident today throughout the United States. California, Louisiana, New Mexico, Nevada, Texas, Arizona, Colorado, and Florida were all once settled by the Spanish. Hispanic-Americans, that is, people whose culture,

Above: **The Spanish established several missions in Arizona, including the Mission of San Xavier del Bac in Tucson. Also known as the White Dove of the Desert, the present building was completed in 1797.**

language, and ethnic identity are rooted in Spain, will soon form the largest ethnic minority in the United States. Most Hispanic-Americans trace their roots back to Latin American countries that were once Spain's New World colonies. Their heritage is evident in their language, Spanish, and in their religion, Roman Catholicism. The Spanish-speaking community in the United States is very large, and most schools have Spanish language classes.

Some cities, such as Santa Barbara in California, still celebrate their Spanish heritage. An Old Spanish Days fiesta is held annually, and townspeople dress in traditional Spanish costumes for the celebrations, which include music, singing, and flamenco dancing. The fame of flamenco dance has spread, and flamenco dance classes are taught in many dance schools across North America. Spanish restaurants and tapas bars are popular entertainment spots.

Today, Spain and the United States cooperate on various cultural and political exchanges. Students visit each other's country on academic exchanges, and a joint commission provides counseling on U.S. educational opportunities to Spanish students.

CITY OF ANGELS

The names of many of the towns in California — San Diego, Santa Barbara, Los Angeles, Monterey, San Francisco — are Spanish names. Los Angeles was originally named *El Pueblo de Nuestra Señora la Reina de Los Angeles*, or The Town of Our Lady the Queen of the Angels.

Below: Olvera Street was once the center of Spanish settlement in Los Angeles. Today, it is the center for Los Angeles' Hispanic community. The city is home to the largest Hispanic community in the United States.

The Spanish–American War

Spanish presence in Latin America eventually led to direct conflict with the United States. In the summer of 1898, the United States fought Spain in one of the shortest and most one-sided wars in modern history. As a result of the Spanish–American War, the United States became a world power that controlled territories from the Caribbean Sea to the western Pacific.

The war started with Cuba's struggle for independence from Spain in 1895. The American public's sympathies for Cubans were aroused. The United States sent the battleship *Maine* to Cuba to protect American interests as anti-Spanish rioting increased. On the night of February 15, 1898, a mysterious explosion destroyed the *Maine*. The crisis rapidly led to the Spanish–American War, declared on April 24, 1898.

The war was conducted both in the Caribbean and in the Philippines. Spain was not equipped, however, to conduct a major naval battle against the United States. The United States had four new battleships in the North Atlantic. Its Asian fleet, under the command of Commodore George Dewey, easily outclassed the

Below: **Spain lost the Spanish–American War in 1898 and was forced to give up the last of its colonial empire.**

old-fashioned Spanish ships based in Manila in the Philippines. In the early dawn of May 1, the American battleships attacked the Spanish fleet. Victory took just a few short hours, and Commander Dewey did not lose a single ship or crew member.

In the Caribbean, the U.S. North Atlantic squadron blockaded the Spanish ships in Santiago harbor, Cuba. Meanwhile, a second party under Theodore Roosevelt advanced on Santiago over land to force the fleet out. The Spanish ships were destroyed or beached by American gunfire as they tried to get out of the harbor. American losses were few in comparison.

On July 18, Spain asked France to help negotiate a peace settlement. The fighting had lasted only about ten weeks. Formal peace talks took place in Paris. Spain granted Cuba its independence, and the United States was given Puerto Rico and Guam. Spain sold the Philippines to the United States for $20 million. It took a three-year guerrilla war, however, for the United States to keep its hold on the Philippines. Moreover, by moving forcefully into the Pacific, the United States placed itself in direct competition with the rising Asian power, Japan. This competition ultimately led to direct, bloody conflict in World War II.

Above: **El Morro was the Spanish fort in San Juan, the capital of Puerto Rico. Puerto Rico was given to the United States after the Spanish–American War and now has commonwealth status.**

Current Relations with the United States

Spain and the United States consider themselves close allies and trading partners today. The two nations cooperate closely as members of NATO and have worked together in peacekeeping operations in Bosnia. Spain allows some of its military facilities to support operations of U.S. forces. The American Naval Station in Rota, Spain, opened in the early 1950s and has developed into one of the most modern, advanced naval installations in the world.

Spain and the United States also cooperate economically and culturally. During Prime Minister José María Aznar's U.S. visit in 1997, the two governments announced a series of new programs for educational exchanges. They also cooperate on an annual Fulbright academic exchange as well as science research programs. On the economic front, U.S. companies are important investors in Spain, and the presence of Spanish investment in the United States is growing. American and Spanish companies are also pursuing joint ventures in fields such as telecommunications and banking. Spain's exports to the United States include textiles, machinery, shoes, fruits and vegetables, and other food products.

Below: **NATO leaders, including President Bill Clinton of the United States** *(far left)* **and Prime Minister José María Aznar of Spain** *(far right),* **gathered for a NATO summit in Madrid in July 1997.**

King Juan Carlos I of Spain Center

IN RECOGNITION OF THE GENEROSITY
AND COMMITMENT OF

FOUNDING MEMBERS OF
THE PATRONATO OF THE
KING JUAN CARLOS I OF SPAIN CENTER
OF NEW YORK UNIVERSITY FOUNDATION

HIS MAJE... JUAN CARLOS I, KING OF SPAIN
HONOR... ...ESIDENT

DR. JO... ...EMAS
FOUN... ...RESIDENT

DR. ... ...A
...EW YORK UNIVERSITY

... DE PRADO Y
...ARVAJAL

...AINZ MUÑOZ
...N SECRETARY

FOUNDING BENI...

CAJA DE AHORR...
FUNDACIÓN CO...
THE COCA-COLA...
GRUPO ENDESA...
IBERDROLA, S.A.
FUNDACIÓN RA...
FUNDACIÓN TAB...
TELEFÓNICA DE...

CAIXA D'ESTALV...
RENFE
MORGAN STAN...

To help stimulate stronger unofficial ties, the American and Spanish governments organized two U.S.–Spain Forums in Seville (1995) and Toledo (1996). This led to the founding of the U.S.-Spain Council, a permanent body consisting of prominent representatives of the business sector, academia, the media, and government from both countries.

Relations with Canada

Spain and Canada are also trading partners and allies in NATO. Spain imports vegetables, paper products, electrical machinery, and metal ores from Canada. It exports railway and transport vehicles, chemicals, mineral fuels, fruit and vegetables, and footwear.

Although political relations between Spain and Canada have remained essentially friendly, they became strained in 1995 over what has been dubbed "The Great Turbot War." Canada was concerned about overfishing of turbot, a species of fish. On March 1995, a Canadian patrol boat arrested a Spanish trawler, accusing the trawler of illegal fishing. Charges were eventually dropped, but the case continues; Spain has brought an action against Canada for boarding and arresting their ship in international waters.

Above: **In 1997, King Juan Carlos** *(right)*, **Queen Sofia** *(center)*, **and First Lady Hillary Clinton** *(left)* **participated in the opening of the Juan Carlos Center for Spanish Studies at New York University. NYU is the first institution in the United States fully dedicated to the study of contemporary Spain. Civic groups also recognized the king for his historic role in support of democracy and human rights.**

Making Their Mark

Further links between Spain and North America have been forged by many famous personalities. Ernest Hemingway (1899–1961), an American writer, was fascinated with Spain and spent many years there. His 1926 novel, *The Sun Also Rises*, made the running of the bulls in Pamplona famous. He was also a war correspondent in the Spanish Civil War and raised money for the army against General Francisco Franco. He wrote *For Whom the Bell Tolls* about his experiences in the conflict, and it became one of his most successful books.

The Spanish actor Antonio Banderas has become very successful in the United States. He was born José Antonio Dominguez Banderas in Málaga, Spain, on August 10, 1960. He starred in many Spanish films before making his American film debut in the 1992 release, *Mambo Kings*. At the time, Banderas knew only a handful of English words, but through eight hours a day of English lessons, he learned the language to the point of dreaming in English. He is married to American actress Melanie Griffith.

The singer Julio Iglesias has been immensely popular for many years. He was born in Madrid on September 23, 1943. A remarkable soccer athlete, he played as goalkeeper and was about

Above, left: Antonio Banderas, a Spanish actor, starred in the 1998 film *The Mask of Zorro.*

Above, right: Julio Iglesias has been singing Latin pop songs since the late 1960s. He sings not only in Spanish and English, but also in German, Japanese, Italian, Portuguese, and French! He is in the *Guinness Book of Records* for having sold over 100 million albums in six languages.

to make his debut in the Real Madrid team. A car accident in 1963, however, left him semi-paralyzed for a year and a half. The nurse who took care of him gave him a guitar. He started to write his own songs and eventually was encouraged to sing them. He has gone on to become a very successful singer of romantic songs, both in Spanish and in English.

Plácido Domingo and José Carreras are two very famous Spanish opera stars. Domingo was born on January 23, 1941, in Madrid, but his family moved to Mexico when he was a child. Today, he is one of the leading tenors in the music world. He has performed all over the world and is a regular performer with the Metropolitan Opera in New York City. José Carreras was born on December 5, 1947 in Barcelona. He and Plácido Domingo joined forces with the Italian singer Luciano Pavarotti in 1990 to form the world-famous group The Three Tenors. This trio has performed on almost every continent.

Below: **The Spanish opera stars José Carreras** *(left)* **and Plácido Domingo** *(center)* **have teamed with Italian singer Luciano Pavarotti** *(right)*, **performing as The Three Tenors.**

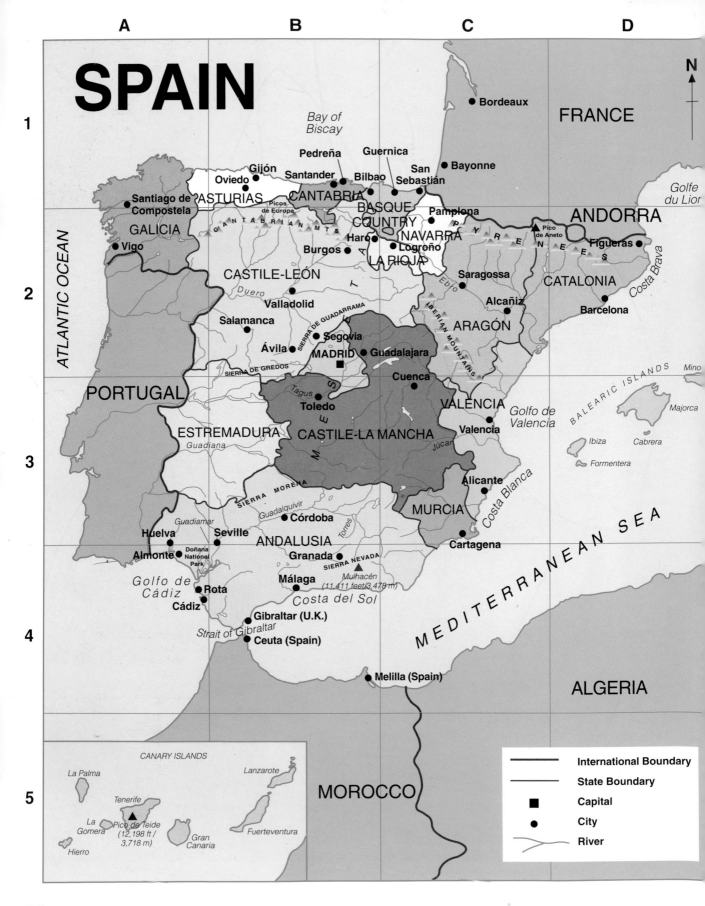

SPAIN

Alcañiz C2
Algeria D4
Alicante C3
Almonte A4
Andalusia B3–B4
Andorra D2
Aragón C2
Asturias B1
Atlantic Ocean A2
Ávila B2

Balearic Islands D3
Barcelona D2
Basque Country C1–C2
Bay of Biscay B1
Bayonne C1
Bilbao B1
Bordeaux C1
Burgos B2

Cabrera D3
Cádiz A4
Canary Islands A5
Cantabria B1
Cantabrian Mts. B2
Cartagena C3
Castile-La Mancha
    B3–C3
Castile-León B2
Catalonia D2
Ceuta B4
Córdoba B3
Costa Blanca C3
Costa Brava D2
Costa del Sol B4
Cuenca C3

Doñana National Park A4
Duero River B2

Ebro River C2
Estremadura A3–B3

Figueras D2
Formentera D3
France D1
Fuerteventura B5

Galicia A1–A2
Gibraltar B4
Gijón B1
Golfe du Lion D1–D2
Golfo de Cádiz A4
Golfo de Valencia C3
Gran Canaria A5
Granada B4
Guadalajara B2
Guadalquivir River B3
Guadiamar River A4
Guadiana River A3–B3
Guernica C1

Haro B2
Hierro A5

Above: The dragon tree *(right)* is native to the Canary Islands.

Huelva A3

Iberian Mountains C2
Ibiza D3

Júcar River C3

La Gomera A5
La Palma A5
La Rioja C2
Lanzarote B5
Logroño C2

Madrid B2
Majorca D3
Málaga B4
Mediterranean Sea
    B4–D4
Melilla B4
Meseta B2–B3
Minorca D3
Morocco B5
Mulhacén B4
Murcia C3

Navarra C2

Oviedo B1

Pamplona C2

Pedreña B1
Pico de Aneto C2
Pico de Teide A5
Picos de Europa B2
Portugal A3
Pyrenees C2–D2

Salamanca B2
San Sebastían C1
Santander B1
Santiago de Compostela
    A1
Saragossa C2
Segovia B2
Seville B3

Sierra de Gredos B2
Sierra de Guadarrama B2
Sierra Morena B3
Sierra Nevada B4
Strait of Gibraltar B4

Tagus River B3
Tenerife A5
Toledo B3
Torres River B4

Valencia (region) C3
Valencia (town) C3
Valladolid B2
Vigo A2

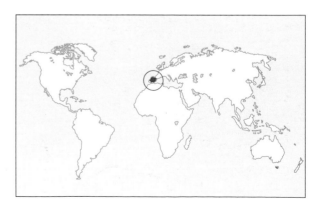

SPAIN

How Is Your Geography?

Learning to identify the main geographical areas and points of a country can be challenging. Although it may seem difficult at first to memorize the locations and spellings of major cities or the names of mountain ranges, rivers, deserts, lakes, and other prominent physical features, the end result of this effort can be very rewarding. Places you previously did not know existed will suddenly come to life when referred to in world news, whether in newspapers, television reports, or other books and reference sources. This knowledge will make you feel a bit closer to the rest of the world, with its fascinating variety of cultures and physical geography.

Used in a classroom setting, the instructor can make duplicates of this map using a copy machine. (PLEASE DO NOT WRITE IN THIS BOOK!) Students can then fill in any requested information on their individual map copies. Used one-on-one, the student can also make copies of the map on a copy machine and use them as a study tool. The student can practice identifying place names and geographical features on his or her own.

Above: **A woman in Galicia.**

Spain at a Glance

Official Name	Kingdom of Spain
Capital	Madrid
Official Language	Castilian Spanish
Population	40 million (2000 estimate)
Land Area	194,898 square miles (504,785 squar e km)
Regions	Andalusia, Aragón, Asturias, Balearic Islands, Basque Country, Canary Islands, Cantabria, Castile-La Mancha, Castile-León, Catalonia, Estremadura, Galicia, La Rioja, Madrid, Murcia, Navarra, Valencia
Highest Point	On continental Spain: Pico de Mulhacén 11,411 feet (3,478 m)
	On Spanish territory: Pico de Teide on Tenerife Island in the Canary Islands 12,198 feet (3,718 m)
Major Rivers	Duero, Ebro, Guadalquivir, Guadiana, Tagus
Main Religion	Roman Catholicism
Major Cities	Barcelona, Madrid, Málaga, Saragossa, Seville, Valencia
Regional Languages	Catalan, Gallego, Euskera
Famous Leaders	Isabella I (1451–1504)
	Charles V (1500–1558)
	General Francisco Franco (1892–1975)
	King Juan Carlos (b. 1938)
Festivals	Carnival, Fallas, Feria de Abril, Rocío, San Fermin, Holy Week
National Anthem	"March of the Royal Grenadier"
Main Imports	Machinery, mineral fuels, vehicles, food
Main Exports	Cars, machinery, metals, chemicals, minerals, textiles, and foodstuffs, including olives and olive oil, wine, and grains
Currency	Spanish Peseta (184.4 pesetas = U.S. $1 as of 2000)

Opposite: **Windmills are part of the landscape at Lanzarote Island, one of the Canary Islands.**

Glossary

Spanish Vocabulary

alcazares (al-kah-THA-res): fortified palaces built by the Moors.

ali-oli (AH-lee OH-lee): garlic and olive oil sauce from Catalonia.

cante (KAHN-teh): flamenco song.

chilindrones (chil-in-DRON-es): marinade sauces from the Pyrenees.

churros (CHEW-ros): sugared strips of fried dough.

fabada (fah-BAH-dah): a stew from the region of Asturias.

ferias (feh-REE-uhs): popular fairs.

fiesta brava (fee-ES-tah BRAH-vah): celebration of bravery.

fronton (fron-TOHN): three-sided court used in the game of jai alai.

jai alai (HYE a-LYE): literally meaning "merry festival," a ball game originating in the Basque region.

montera (mon-TEH-rah): wide-brimmed hat worn by matadors during the opening ceremony of bullfights.

paella (pie-AY-yah): a dish of rice with seafood or meat.

pasos (PAH-sohs): floats used in Holy Week processions, bearing life-size statues of Jesus or Mary.

pelota vasca (peh-LOH-tah VAS-kah): another name for the game of jai alai.

romerías (rom-er-EE-ahs): religious pilgrimages in Spain.

sangría (sang-GREE-ya): red wine mixed with fruit and soda water.

tapas (TAH-pahs): Spanish appetizers or snacks.

English Vocabulary

annex: to take or add on something, such as a territory.

autonomous: self-governing.

barricade: a defensive barrier.

Berbers: a group of people in North Africa.

bodega: a wine cellar.

carcass: the body of a dead animal.

castanets: a small percussion instrument consisting of two round shells of wood that are held in the hand and clicked rhythmically together. They are used by flamenco dancers.

concessions: something granted by a government, such as land or privileges.

corral: an enclosure or pen for animals such as bulls or horses.

cove: a small indentation in the shoreline of a sea, lake, river, or ocean.

cubism: a style of painting or sculpture in which objects are reduced to their geometrical features.

dexterity: skill with the body or hands.

dour: gloomy, sullen.

enclave: a country or a portion of a country surrounded by foreign territory.

estuary: mouth of a river where it meets the sea.

Eucharist: the sacrament of the Holy Communion.

Euskara: the language spoken by the Basque people.

expulsion: forcing out.

fatalities: deaths.

Gallego: also known as Galician; the language spoken in Galicia.

Hispaniola Island: the island in the West Indies consisting of Haiti and the Dominican Republic.

Holy Roman Emperor: this title was first given to a king by the pope in Rome in A.D. 800. The title of Holy Roman Emperor was borne by German kings until 1806. Their control extended over much of Western Europe (including Spain), but their empire is not related to the Roman Empire of earlier centuries.

Iberian Peninsula: the peninsula of southwestern Europe occupied by Spain and Portugal.

invincible: something that cannot be defeated.

isthmus: a narrow strip of land connecting two large bodies of land and bordered by water.

laden: burdened.

Latin America: the regions of North and South America in which Spanish, Portuguese, or French is spoken.

Lent: the period of forty days before Easter when Christians fast or give up something special.

literate: able to read and write.

lithograph: a kind of print that uses an inked stone or metal plate.

mariner: sailor; seaman.

matador: a bullfighter.

men-of-war: warships.

meseta: the central plateau of Spain.

mestizo: people of mixed Spanish and native American blood.

minstrel: a medieval poet, singer, or musician.

monarchist: someone in favor of a monarchy in a country.

Moors: the African Arabs and Berbers who ruled Spain from the eighth to the fifteenth century A.D.

NATO: North Atlantic Treaty Organization; a military alliance of Western nations.

New World: North and South America and the surrounding islands; so-named by the early European explorers.

nomadic: moving from place to place rather than being settled in one place.

penitent: (n.) a person who has admitted to a wrongdoing and submits to a punishment by the Church.

pledged: promised.

Protestant Reformation: a movement in the sixteenth century to reform the Roman Catholic Church. It eventually resulted in the establishment of the Protestant churches.

regime: rule.

republic: a state in which the head of government is not a monarch but an elected or nominated president.

republican: someone in favor of a republic.

revered: greatly respected.

Romany: the language spoken by Gypsies.

secular: non-religious.

Semana Santa: Holy Week.

siesta: an afternoon nap.

supremacy: having the highest authority or power.

surrealism: a style of art in which the subconscious is stressed. The imagery is often very fanciful.

treacherous: dangerous.

veneration: to regard with great respect.

virtuoso: a person who has special knowledge or skill in his or her field.

More Books to Read

Country Topics for Craft Projects: Spain. Catherine Chambers (Franklin Watts)

Francisco Goya. Hispanics of Achievement series. Martha Richardson (Chelsea House)

Juan Ponce de León. Sean Dolan (Chelsea House)

Native Americans and the Spanish. Therese De Angelis (Chelsea House)

Passport to Spain. Keith Lye (Franklin Watts)

Salvador Dali. Hispanics of Achievement series. David Carter (Chelsea House)

Spain: Bridge between Continents. Stephen Chicoine (Benchmark Books)

Spain. Country Fact Files series. Anna Selby (Raintree Steck-Vaughn)

Spain. Cultures of the World series. Elizabeth Kohen (Marshall Cavendish)

Spain. Festivals of the World series. Susan McKay (Gareth Stevens)

A Taste of Spain. Bob Goodwin and Candi Perez (Thomson Learning)

Videos

Andrés Segovia: The Song of the Guitar. (Allegro Films/Teldec Video)

Barcelona. (Freelance Video)

The Buried Mirror: Reflections on Spain and the New World. (Public Media Video)

Spain: Madrid and Toledo, Seville and Andalusia. (Small World Productions)

Spain Barcelona Segovia Granada. (Questar)

Web Sites

www.docuweb.ca/SiSpain/

www.clark.net/pub/jumpsam/wwwspain.htm

coloquio.com/index.html

futures.wharton.upenn.edu/~jonath22/gaudi.html

Due to the dynamic nature of the Internet, some web sites stay current longer than others. To find additional web sites, use a reliable search engine with one or more of the following keywords to help you locate information about Spain. Keywords: *Andalusia, Basques, bullfighting, flamenco, Madrid, Picasso, Seville, Spain, Spanish.*

Index